marriage counseling in GROUPS

Merle M. Ohlsen

Research Press Company

2612 North Mattis Avenue
Champaign, Illinois 61820

Cover design and illustrations by Bob Harvey.

Copies of this book may be ordered from the publisher at the address given on the title page.

ISBN 0-87822-201-4

Library of Congress Catalog Card Number 79-66180

To Helen—wonderful lover, partner, and friend

Contents

Preface

I wrote this book to help marriage counselors improve their understanding of their clients and the therapeutic forces within a marriage counseling group, to use these forces productively, to help clients recognize and accept responsibility for their own growth, to facilitate clients' success in achieving their own goals, and to encourage clients to continue their growth subsequent to counseling. Case materials are used to alert counselors to the natural consequences that result when either a client resists change or the counselor fails to act or acts inappropriately or unethically.

On the other hand, I have tried to present my ideas in language from which persons who are not qualified marriage counselors can profit: couples who are looking for ideas which they can use to enrich their relationship; couples in counseling for whom their counselors or therapists believe their growth could be enhanced by self-help materials; clergy and divorce lawyers who recognize that they are not qualified counselors but wish to improve their conferences with couples and make better referrals.

In addition to making a conscientious effort to review the relevant literature and research findings from group dynamics, social psychology, group counseling, group psychotherapy, and marriage and family counseling, I have tried to draw upon my graduate teaching, practicum supervision, and counseling experiences to suggest how to apply this knowledge in marriage and family counseling.

Throughout this book I encourage counselors to obtain the best possible preparation and to accept responsibility for their continuing growth in practice. In order for counselors to provide quality services they must be committed professionals who are able to appraise their clients' progress, be willing to terminate and/or refer those who fail to make normal progress in achieving their goals, and be willing to seek supervision to ensure their continuing professional development. Only those who are most competent should be encouraged to remain in the profession.

Truth in packaging is stressed. Marriage counselors are encouraged to describe for prospective clients what will be expected of them and what they can expect from other clients and the counselor, to answer prospective clients' questions concerning the counseling process, the counselor's qualifications, and the outcomes of counseling, and to help them decide whether or not to contract for marriage counseling. Clients are encouraged to explore how this temporary helping relationship differs from their continuing relationship with significant others and why they must complete their unfinished business with significant others.

I emphasize the importance of the counselor teaching each client to accept responsibility for his decisions and his own growth. In addition to helping clients decide for themselves whether or not marriage counseling is appropriate for them, they are taught to recognize their own pain and self-defeating behaviors, to discuss them openly, to solicit feedback from fellow clients, to define precise behavioral goals, to define criteria which they can use to appraise their own growth, and to solicit encouragement and reinforcement from their significant others.

I am most grateful to all those clients, graduate students, and colleagues who have provided me with feedback, challenged me, and helped me to develop and clarify my counseling techniques.

Introduction

This book describes the counseling process. It explains why a counselor who follows the procedures endorsed in this book selects his clients and prepares them for counseling with such care, tells how he selects his clients, and describes how he helps them in groups. In fact, most counselors who elect to help reasonably healthy clients and prefer to give their clients maximum responsibility for discussing where they hurt, for discovering their self-defeating behaviors, for learning new coping behaviors, for defining the new behavior that they would like to learn, and for implementing their desired new behaviors can apply the techniques described in this book. A variety of case materials are used to illustrate typical sources of pain for couples who seek marital counseling, how different techniques can be applied to help different types of clients, and how clients can be helped in marriage counseling groups.

Clients have learned to be what they are. Some of their learning is incomplete. They have not learned to cope adequately with some of the problems they face by mastering necessary developmental tasks. Others have learned self-defeating behaviors that they must recognize and replace with more productive behaviors. In both cases they experience some pain. The discussion of this pain can be used to motivate individuals to define desired new behaviors, to practice them, to develop the courage and self-confidence to implement these new behaviors, to implement them, and to seek encouragement and reinforcement for these new behaviors from significant others.

Counselors are encouraged to give their clients maximum responsibility for detecting their own pain, for ascertaining whether or not they require assistance, for defining their goals (desired new behaviors), for implementing their new behaviors, and for ensuring their continuing growth.

In order to encourage a client to accept maximum responsibility, the counselor tries to convey to a prospective client what will be expected from her as a client and as a helper, what she can expect from other members, including the counselor, how she can expect to be helped, and what she can do to get herself ready for counseling, for defining *her own goals*, for facilitating her own and others' growth, and for helping to develop and maintain therapeutic norms in her group. Incidentally, this emphasis on "truth in packaging" and on helping clients earn membership in their counseling group also makes group counseling attractive to prospective clients.

When a client has heard a brief description of the helping process and has observed the counselor answering her questions concerning expectations and the counselor's qualifications in a nondefensive manner, she tends to discuss her pain openly in the intake interview. Whether or not she continues in that vein is determined by the degree to which the counselor listens empathically, expresses genuine caring, manages transference and countertransference well, and relates specific pains to desired new behaviors. Having a clear and satisfactory definition of confidentiality and the rationale for it also contribute to therapeutic talk.

Thus clients do learn to keep confidences and recognize the consequences that result from breaking confidences. They also learn how to deal with the situation when they suspect that someone has broken confidences. On the other hand, each learns with whom he can share what he discusses within his group, how he can share his goals with significant others, and how he may solicit encouragement and support from them. Moreover, some usually require assistance in determining what is reinforcing and encouraging for them and in communicating these discoveries to the relevant others.

During counseling, clients discover that even other clients whom they admire have problems as serious as their own. Furthermore, they are encouraged when they observe these peers achieving their goals.

In most groups there are some clients who tend to look upon themselves as victims of fate. During counseling they usually discover that others like themselves do have some control over their destiny. Thus, they are encouraged to define and implement new behaviors in areas of their lives in which they had tended to perceive themselves as hopelessly trapped.

Finally, clients learn to accept themselves better as they are, to present themselves as they are, and to work for the changes that they desire most. Many conclude that their real selves are much better than any of the facades that they previously tried to wear. Moreover, during the process of being helper as well as client they learn to accept and to enjoy a degree of intimacy that they had never before experienced. They also learn to tolerate, and even to respect, individual differences and values and to accept others' solutions to problems that would be inappropriate for them.

THE COUNSELING SESSION: AN OVERVIEW

Why Group Counseling?

Counseling couples in groups is a recent innovation. Until only a few years ago, most authorities did not endorse counseling husband and wife together (Mittelman, 1944; Papanek, 1971). Today, treatment of couples together is endorsed by most authorities (Gurman & Rice, 1975). Some even believe that treating spouses separately can increase the chances of divorce (Ackerman, 1970). When husband and wife are treated together, each learns to listen, empathize, communicate, and share more spontaneously with the other. Gradually both spouses learn to recognize feelings of annoyance and to deal with them before getting angry. They learn to recognize the clues that suggest a developing conflict, to sort out what is upsetting, to face the conflict, and to deal with it directly. They learn to discuss what they had always thought they could expect from each other, including everything from common everyday expectations to new agreements. Furthermore, they learn to do this in the presence of four other couples who can see through their unproductive games, are able to give helpful feedback that is the result of similar experience, and are even able to insist that they learn to behave more effectively. Within the group they also discover good individual models, learn to use their counseling group as a support group, learn to differentiate a support group from a rescue service, and learn to develop a meaningful support group outside their counseling group. Their faith in learning new behaviors and their success in learning them are substituted for hurtful criticism, fighting, and self-pity. And the growth of others in the group is a further source of encouragement.

Although this book is concerned with counseling couples in groups, most experienced counselors have found that when marriage partners with families have problems, their children may be involved. In these situations there is considerable value in intensive family therapy, too. An individual frequently needs help in understanding how his own and his spouse's family values and lifestyle account for their problems and can be used to solve them (see Chapter 9). Each family member has learned some attitudes, behaviors, and values within the family that enhance effective living and others that don't. The inappropriate ones must be replaced by appropriate ones that will foster more satisfying relationships within the family unit. Some counselors emphasize treating the family as a whole, helping individual members use the positive skills they have learned elsewhere to function better as a group (Dreikurs, 1972; Satir, Stachowiak, & Taschman, 1975). Some counselors stress helping parents accept the primary responsibility for improving their family life.

When a couple needs special help with their child-rearing problems, the counselor organizes new-parent education groups (see Chapter 12). For others he schedules an occasional extra hour of treatment time just prior to the regular counseling session. For these sessions the counselor uses an essentially

Adlerian family counseling model (Dreikurs, 1972). This session is used to help the entire family identify their primary problems, to discuss possible solutions, and to decide what each must do to improve family life. The counselor may also help them decide how to introduce and maintain a family council if they do not already have one. Following the family counseling session, the other four couples encourage the family to discuss what they learned from the session, give feedback to each individual as well as to the family as a group, and help each member make essential commitments to implement agreed upon new behaviors.

The treatment method presented in this book is based on a learning model that helps couples master normal developmental tasks, recognize and prevent, wherever possible, the development of serious problems, spot early symptoms of self-defeating behaviors, and replace these behaviors with desirable ones. Increasingly, marriage counselors are using such educational and preventative models (Olson, 1976). Thus, the trend is for marriage counselors to use the group format to help couples learn specific new relationship skills, practice pro-

posed new behaviors, and solicit feedback on their success with homework assignments. With increased use of such group strategies also has come a shift away from open-ended (and often long-term) treatment to short-term treatment with behavioral contracts (Olson, 1976).

The Group Setting

Effective group counseling for couples doesn't require a great deal of space and equipment. A pleasant, soundproof room, in which clients can talk freely without being overheard by others in surrounding rooms, with space for at least eleven comfortable chairs placed in a circle, is sufficient. Carpeting and enough space for clients to shove the chairs back and sit on the floor or do exercises is very helpful, too. Obviously, the space, equipment, and furnishings suggest the degree to which the institution supports marriage counseling (and the private practitioner's level of success in his practice).

An audio recording system is essential so that clients can review what happened at any given time in a session and can give feedback to one another on role-played sessions. During reviews it is desirable to have a second recorder to tape the discussion of the role-played session. A recording also enables the counselor to obtain feedback from clients or a professional colleague. Video recordings are even better for these purposes because they show unproductive and/or distracting behaviors, encouraging behaviors, and unverbalized needs.

Most counselors and therapists limit their counseling groups to six to eight adults. For marriage counseling groups, however, I select five couples to provide more varied models for couples and individuals to use in learning and implementing new behaviors. The larger group also provides richer feedback to both individuals and couples. Nevertheless, the counselor should watch for signs of the primary dangers of a large counseling group: that clients are having too little meaningful interaction with each other, that they have become too dependent on the counselor, and that they are channeling most communication through the counselor or a group "spokesperson" (Loeser, 1957; Psathas, 1960). In any case, each client and each couple must feel that they are allocated adequate time during each session, that no one has to wait too long to get the floor, and that the group is small enough for each person to get to know the others. Even though smaller groups are easier to manage, the additional models that a larger group provides justify taking on the problems that increased size creates in marriage counseling.

The Therapeutic Triad

Many people feel that it is difficult for three persons to develop an effective working relationship. Even a child discovers early in life to pair up first with one parent, then another, and to play them off against each other. Rather than complaining about or seeking revenge against one's spouse or trying to manipulate the counselor into taking sides and hurting the spouse in some other way, each client must learn to pair up with the counselor and other group members to help her spouse. Each client also must learn to discuss her own problems and to improve herself

So that is how the triad works.
While I am talking, you are Dr.
J's special helper.

rather than to complain about her spouse or to blame him for their marriage problems. Increasingly both spouses realize that each of them is the only person who can really change: he must change himself and she must change herself. And they learn to enlist each other's help in practicing and reinforcing desired new behaviors. When, for example, the wife speaks first during the intake interview (the first meeting between the counselor and the couple), she is encouraged to discuss her own shortcomings and feelings of inadequacy and to develop her own plan for learning positive new behaviors. While she is talking, the counselor listens very carefully. He tries to detect precisely what worries and upsets her; he encourages her to discuss her own pain and to decide exactly what she would like to change to improve herself and helps her define what new behaviors she must learn to function more effectively. In the group he also encourages other clients, especially her husband, to do the same. In particular, he encourages her husband to listen and to support and reinforce these desired new behaviors. Later, especially during the early group sessions, the counselor watches for good helper as well as good client behaviors and calls them to the attention of the other clients to reinforce them and to encourage other clients to emulate them.

Frequently the listening spouse, the husband in the case discussed above, has difficulty listening to his wife. He is tempted to complain about her or to edit what she is saying. When this occurs, the counselor must interrupt the husband and explain how such behavior wastes time and, worse still, can hurt his wife to the point that one or both of them refuse to continue counseling. When, however, the husband becomes aware of a problem that he feels they must begin work on soon and that he thinks may call for his wife to learn some specific new behaviors, he may ask her whether or not she would be willing to consider adding an item to her list of goals. The counselor also can use such an instance to teach other group members as well as the husband the difference between demands and requests. He can help the wife realize that since it is not her own goal, she can decide whether or not she accepts it. Sometimes such a request also opens up opportunities to discuss the natural consequences of refusing to change and, especially, to learn this particular new behavior.

During the intake interview—his first contact with a couple—the counselor helps them discuss briefly what their problems are and what they will require of each other and significant others to solve them. Then the counselor shifts quickly to help each to discuss his own pain and to function as each other's helper. Next the counselor describes the triad, tells how it works, explains why he uses it. He asks them to convince themselves and each other of their mutual commitment to talk openly, to learn desired new behaviors, to help other group members learn new behaviors, and to help them develop and maintain a therapeutic group. Thus, each client is given the responsibility for demonstrating his own readiness to face each of his problems and to learn the necessary new behaviors to solve those problems.

When a prospective client cannot make these commitments, he is helped to explore the consequences of doing nothing at this time and the possibilities for getting help elsewhere. When either party wants revenge, the counselor reflects the impression of this need to the client. Exposing this need tends to be shocking to both spouses, but it also tends to motivate them to complete the unfinished business associated with need for revenge. Other feelings that block making the necessary commitments are general fear of change and fear that willingness to change in the present will call forth more and more demands for change in the future. As each discovers how he is expected to define and implement his own goals, the latter is minimized.

Basic Components in the Counseling Process

Group counseling is basically a self-help process. The individual must *want* to make it work. A willingness to discuss one's problems, a commitment to learn essential new behaviors, a desire to support a therapeutic climate within the group and to encourage others in the group to do the same—these are crucial parts of counseling. Each client must understand the importance of these commitments to insure his own success and that of the group.

The counselor's role is essentially a helping one. He must be able to inspire trust, detect and reflect a clients' pain, and reinforce clients' attempts to try new behaviors. The counselor must be able to implement all the basic components of the counseling process described below and communicate them to the client.

Developing a counseling relationship:
The intake interview and beyond

During the intake interview, a preliminary meeting between the couple and the counselor prior to the first group session, the counselor describes the treatment process, answers their questions concerning expectations and possible benefits, and helps them develop meaningful treatment goals. The counselor's first tasks are to encourage each spouse to discuss what genuinely concerns him or her, to explain what is needed to make counseling most effective, and to convey how important it is that each of them accept responsibility for his own growth and for learning to trust other clients as well as the counselor. The way the counselor answers their questions and responds to their behaviors (including their defensive behaviors) and their reservations can enhance their trust or decrease it. Of course it can be reassuring when a client has heard from others he admires that the counselor is competent and worthy of his trust, but he must also discover from his own experiences with the counselor and the group that she is trustworthy and that she can help the group develop a working climate in which clients can learn to trust each other.

Once the counselor has explained the ground rules, she encourages the client to talk about what really worries and upsets him *about himself.* Most people who seek counseling are ready to discuss their own pain, but some begin by complaining about their spouses. When a client does not discuss where *he* hurts, the counselor repeats her description of the counseling process and its related expectations—among them the expectation that each client come to the first group session prepared to discuss his most painful feelings and do it.

Shyness, lack of trust, and doubts about being able to be helped can inhibit therapeutic talk. Sometimes it helps to have the reluctant client tell the counselor why some painful topics are so threatening or embarrassing. In any case, he must be helped to face and discuss his own pain and to decide what he wants to do about it. The counselor can facilitate this process by trying to guess precisely what his client's pain is by using accurate reflections to encourage open discussion and to relate his pain to desired new behaviors.

Burt, a healthy twenty-three-year-old, was obviously embarrassed when he began the intake interview. After he complained angrily about his wife's housekeeping and cooking, he became very quiet and seemed to be near tears.

The counselor said, "Things are going very badly with your wife. Perhaps she is even more disappointed with you than you are with her."

All Burt said was, "Yes, even worse than you'd guess."

There was another long pause, and the counselor said, "Perhaps it would help if you could tell me why it is so embarrassing and why, perhaps, you doubt that even I could understand the problem."

Burt's response was, "Right."

After another pause the counselor said, "Try me. There is no other way. Tell me now, and I will suffer with you, help you face your pain, and help you decide what you can do about it." Ever so slowly he talked about his impotence and about his fears of losing his wife. Very reluctantly he agreed to bring his wife along the next time and to enlist her help in solving their problems.

Before Burt left, the counselor helped him decide how he would ask his wife to come back with him, how he would tell her why he wanted her help, what he felt their major problems were, and what additional assistance might be needed. Then the counselor had him role play how he would ask his wife about helping him. This practice session was recorded, and the counselor helped him to critique it. Although Burt was not certain that she would come with him to the next session, she did. She listened and appeared to be committed to making their marriage successful.

Burt's case is a good example of client preparation for counseling. The counselor does everything he can to earn the client's trust, but at some point the client must simply accept the responsibility for learning to trust and begin to talk about his most painful feelings. This kind of forthright dealing can be scary, but it is the necessary first step every client must take. The first client to do this during the first group session usually feels intense pressure, but after she has done it, she feels relieved and glad that she found the courage early. The payoff comes when she gets increased help and respect from others in the group. Also, the counselor watches for and points out the payoffs to other clients. On the other hand, when clients fail to discuss their problems openly and don't become meaningfully involved early in the life of the group, they tend to either drop out or become nonparticipants (Sethna & Harrington, 1971).

The group can enhance clients' willingness to talk openly since openness is learned from peers more easily than from the counselors. As laypersons, group members provide un-censored, more realistic responses. Peers' feedback is less threatening and, hence, brings forth a less defensive response. Group members more readily accept one anothers' problems and offer reasonable assistance (Beck, 1958). Clients are also relieved to discover that others have problems as difficult as theirs and are encouraged by other clients' confidence that they can learn desired new behaviors. Consequently, they develop a sense of belonging that is equally essential for those who wish to change and for those who wish to help them change (Cartwright, 1951). Sharing problems increases clients' identification with others in the group and enhances their com-mitment to learn desired new behaviors (Kelman, 1963). This feeling is further reinforced when the counselor points out sim-ilarities among individuals' problems and encourages those who have had success to help others with similar problems.

Detecting a client's problem

In order to detect a client's pain and to understand it ade-quately, the counselor must try to sense precisely what her client is feeling. Knowing the client's feelings enables the coun-selor to respond in ways that facilitate open discussion of his pain. Although external sources of data, such as interviews with relatives and friends, can provide important information, most counselors help the client learn to present his own back-ground. They watch the way he struggles with painful topics. The way a client approaches and pulls back from certain topics, his speech patterns, facial expressions, posturing, movements, nonverbal communication of emotions, and use of emotionally loaded words can provide important behavioral clues. However, competent counselors realize that different people may express different feelings with similar behavior. For example, some people tease and use sarcastic remarks to convey affection that they are reluctant or unable to com-municate directly. When some people feel hostile, they act bored or indifferent or defensive. Thus, counselors recognize that in order to detect and respond to a client's real feelings, they must know something about a client's lifestyle, values, and ways of communicating emotions.

Reflecting a client's feelings. Today, most counselors and therapists place less emphasis on why the client feels and behaves as he does and more emphasis on exposing the client's underlying feelings and using them as energy to facilitate implementing a client's desired new behaviors. In other words, they use less interpretation and more reflection. However, to use either, a counselor must be able to detect the client's pain and to express her understandings to the client.

Two primary distinctions differentiate interpretation from reflection: one, the extent to which the counselor assumes the role of expert and two, the extent to which the counselor assumes responsibility for her client. For example, the following response to Burt is an interpretation: "The first time that your wife suggested intercourse and you could not have an erection, and she laughed, you were very embarrassed, but you were unable to share your embarrassment. Instead of sharing it, you reacted with anger and said that you were turned off by her fat." In this instance, the counselor has assumed the expert role and perhaps unknowingly has made the client more dependent by explaining the situation to him. This kind of response might work with some people, but many clients tend to perceive interpretation as attack or a putdown (Ohlsen, 1977).

Instead of *explaining why* the client felt as he did in that instance, the counselor could have used a reflection to encourage the client to discuss his feelings of inadequacy and embarrassment. This tactic could have opened up possibilities for the client to relate his pain to wished-for new behaviors. Thus, instead of giving Burt an answer, the counselor might have said, "She really hurt you. Perhaps you'd like to talk to your wife about that embarrassing moment, but you don't know how or where to begin." This kind of response conveys understanding, compassion, and a willingness to help the client learn to cope with his problem. It possibly even communicates some hope and shared responsibility for planning action. The counselor touches base with the client, and encourages him to discuss his pain and do something about it. Such reflections tend to be most productive when they focus a little ahead of and a little deeper than where the client was when he spoke.

Some clients may not realize what a counselor is doing when he first uses a reflection. When, therefore, he first uses this technique, he may have to explain why he is doing so. Following the effective use of a reflection he may make a response such as "That is not the kind of response you'd expect in social conversation and you wonder what I am up to. It's a reflection. Let me try to explain what makes it an effective technique. You should know that I only use it when I have a hunch where I think you are hurting and am confident that you can cope with the underlying pain you are experiencing. In other words, it is an encouraging response and an expression of faith in your ability to solve this problem. I will teach all of you to use it to help each other in our group."

Relating pain to behavioral goals. As the counselor listens to a client discuss his pain, she tries to decide when it is time to use another reflection. Again she makes guesses, such as "Perhaps now you wish to talk to Burt about . . . and to your mother about. . . ."

The timing of such a second reflection is very important. The counselor must be able to sense when the client has had the right amount of time to discuss his feelings. If the counselor or another group member breaks in too soon, the speaker may feel that they don't know enough to help or are tired of listening. On the other hand, if the speaker is permitted to talk about his pain too long, he will experience some relief from catharsis and lose some of his motivation to complete unfinished business—to learn essential new behaviors.

Early in the life of the group, a counselor can use one member's shared problems, pain, and goals to teach others in the group to use reflections to relate their pain to their desired new behavior (goals). She should explain why it is better for other group members rather than the counselor or spouse to pressure the client into practicing (role playing) a new behavior in the group and, eventually, implementing it between counseling sessions. After another group member pressures a client, the counselor says, "So now you realize that you have to. . . . With whom could you practice that in here now? What help will you require of your husband (wife) when you put these ideas into practice before we have our next session?"

Defining criteria. An important part of solving a problem is defining goals. Clients need clear, precise behavioral goals.

A client may begin with large, long-term goals that can be broken up into specific, short-term goals. Once these are established, the client can decide whose help he will need to implement and/or reinforce them. Sometimes a counselor does not realize the degree to which he is accepting vague, general goals until he begins to help his client define criteria for appraising achievement of the client's goals. The following kinds of questions can be used to sharpen goals:

- How will you know when you have achieved it?
- How will you feel or behave differently?
- What new behaviors will the significant others in your life notice?
- How will they recognize the new behaviors that you want them to reinforce to ensure your continued growth?

Discussion of such questions enables the client to develop and add specific criteria he can use to appraise his own progress. Perhaps nothing is more encouraging (and more reinforcing) for a client than to discover the clear evidence of his own growth that specific criteria measure.

Precise criteria counteract the tendency for the members of a client's family to reinforce old, deviant behaviors (Liberman, 1970). These criteria can also be used by the counselor to determine whether a client is being helped by a particular treatment or whether a different method of treatment or, perhaps, a different counselor would be in the client's best interest.

Defining mini-goals.   Most clients begin to state objectives by defining broad, general goals. Once goals have been defined, the client must break them into mini-goals—behaviors that she can arrange in a hierarchy. Other group members are often quite helpful as the client develops the hierarchy and decides with which goal and which person she can begin.

Teaching clients to be clients and helpers

The better that clients understand and accept what they must do to achieve their own goals and to help others achieve theirs, the more effective the group tends to be. When a counselor describes a marriage counseling group to a couple and answers their questions about it, he has begun the process of teaching them to be clients and helpers. The counselor can reinforce a client who, in the early stages of the group, is functioning well as either a client or helper by pointing out the productive behavior to others in the group. This strategy provides clients with a good, living model. (By encouraging clients to watch for good client and helper behaviors and reinforcing them, a client can increase the productivity of the group, too.) Nevertheless, in spite of the explanations and living examples, almost every client at some point will wonder what to do. At such times the counselor should encourage the client to ask what he needs to know—or at least to admit that he does not know what to do or how to do it. Rather than immediately springing to the client's aid, the counselor should determine whether another client can explain what to do or, better still, demonstrate what to do. Clients can also learn from video recordings of the early sessions of other groups. Of course, permission from the individuals involved is necessary.

Learning interpersonal skills. Frequently, a client needs new skills to implement new behaviors he has selected. Films and video recordings can be used effectively to help him learn these skills, but role playing tends to be more effective for this purpose (see Chapter 6). During the process of describing his situation, selecting the cast of role players from the group, and preparing them for their roles, the client acquires new insights into his situation and increased empathy for the significant others involved in the real life situation.

Soliciting feedback on successes and failures. When clients are encouraged to practice their new behaviors between sessions, they need feedback on their *successes* as well as failures. Feedback on failures (negative feedback) can be used to develop new coping strategies, while positive feedback can be used as a basis from which to generalize and apply past successes to new settings. Clients also enjoy learning to celebrate their successes.

Helping the counselor manage his own feelings
Good counselors need feedback, too, and one good source of feedback is clients. When a counselor solicits feedback from his clients, he should give them some idea of the kind of information he finds most helpful. The following questions help clients focus their analysis:
1. Where was I, or the group, especially helpful?
2. Where was I, or the group, hurtful?

3. What specifically did we do that helped or hurt you?
4. How do you wish that we would have behaved differently?

This kind of feedback is especially helpful in keeping the counselor in touch with his own feelings, values, and unsolved problems. When he is functioning at his best, he is able to listen to a client, help her discuss what is important to her, decide what is the best solution for her, and keep his own values and unsolved problems from interfering with his effectiveness. It is important that the counselor recognize when he is distracted by his own unsolved problems, especially when those problems are similar to or related to the client's. Sometimes he may even have to admit that he is distracted and requires extra help from other group members. He also can ask himself why the client's problems make it difficult for him to give her his very best assistance and how he can use these feelings to detect her pain and reflect it most accurately. On such occasions he also should seek feedback on a recording of that session from a respected professional. These steps will ensure that each client is given the best possible opportunity to profit from counseling.

Summary

In order for marriage counseling to be most effective, individuals must be able and committed to discuss their own pain openly rather than to complain about their spouse, to define and implement desired new behaviors, and to help other group members do the same. Starting with the first session, everyone must be willing to accept his own pain and discuss it. Whenever one is confronted with doubts concerning what is expected of him or whether he can trust some other member, he is encouraged to discuss his sources of doubt and threat with the relevant person or persons. In addition to enabling each person to feel good about the genuineness of others in the group, couples learn to face their difficulties, to master conflict resolution skills, to obtain feedback, including reinforcement for being frank and considerate, from others in the group, and to experience some personal good feelings from their successes. Thus, even before clients decide to join a counseling group they have a clear notion of what to expect; they are helped to accept responsibility for their own growth.

Questions to Think About

1. As a counselor, how would you determine whether or not the members of the group understand what is expected of them?
2. What are the primary advantages and disadvantages of treating husband and wife in the same group?
3. How may a counselor use group members' responses to each other to enhance therapeutic talk in a group?
4. What criteria would you use to determine whether a client's talk is therapeutic or not?
5. Why is it advisable for a counselor to use a reflection rather than an interpretation?
6. Why should the counselor detect the *precise* nature of the client's pain and use reflection to uncover it and relate it to specific new behaviors?
7. What is the primary danger of allowing a client to talk out his problems too thoroughly before helping him to define goals and to focus on implementing them during the first session?
8. Under what circumstances can feedback be best heard and used to implement new behaviors?
9. What might you do to encourage a client to accept responsibility for his own growth?
10. Assuming that you are dissatisfied with your marriage and are satisfied that you have selected a competent counselor, to what questions would you require answers in order to determine whether or not marriage counseling was worth the time, effort, and money required to achieve successful results?
11. What happens when a member of a group fails to self-disclose during the first several sessions of a marriage counseling group?

References

Ackerman, N. W. *Family therapy in transition*. Boston: Little, Brown, 1970.

Beck, D. F. The dynamics of group psychotherapy as seen by a sociologist. *Sociometry*, 1958, *21*, 98–128, 180–197.

Cartwright, D. Achieving change in people: Some applications of group dynamics theory. *Human Relations*, 1951, *4*, 381–392.

Dreikurs, R. Family counseling: A demonstration. *Journal of Individual Psychology*, 1972, *28*, 207–222.

Gurman, A. S., & Rice, D. G. *Couples in conflict*. New York: Jason Aronson, 1975.

Kelman, H. C. The role of the group in the induction of therapeutic change. *International Journal of Group Psychotherapy*, 1963, *13*, 399–442.

Liberman, R. L. Behavioral approaches to family and couple therapy. *American Journal of Orthopsychiatry*, 1970, *40*, 106–118.

Loeser, L. Some aspects of group dynamics. *International Journal of Psychotherapy*, 1957, *7*, 7–19.

Mittelman, B. Complementary neurotic reactions in intimate relationships. *Psychoanalytic Quarterly*, 1944, *13*, 479–485.

Ohlsen, M. M. *Group counseling*. New York: Holt, Rinehart and Winston, 1977.

Olson, D. H. (Ed.). *Treating relationships*. Lake Mills, Ia.: Graphic Publishing Co., 1976.

Papanek, H. Group therapy with married couples. In H. I. Kaplan & B. J. Sadoch (Eds.), *Psychotherapy*. Baltimore: Wilkins & Wilkins, 1971.

Psathas, G. Phase, movement and equilibrium tendencies in interaction process in psychotherapy groups. *Sociometry*, 1960, *33*, 171–194.

Satir, V., Stachowiak, J., & Taschman, H. A. *Helping families to change*. New York: Jason Aronson, 1975.

Sethna, E. R., & Harrington, J. A. A study of patients who lapsed from group therapy. *British Journal of Psychiatry*, 1971, *119*, 59–69.

2

WHO NEEDS IT?

With the social changes that are occurring today added to their normal marriage problems, more and more people are recognizing the need for marriage counseling. Somewhere between 40 and 60 percent of all couples require marrige counseling (Otto, 1976.) At least half of the married couples in this country have some sexual dysfunctioning problem (Masters & Johnson, 1975). Even couples who have good marriages are seeking counseling in order to improve their marriage relationships. Church-related organizations are providing couples with new opportunities to participate in parent education programs, in marriage enrichment programs, and in marriage counseling. Personal growth courses, workshops, and retreats have awakened people to realize the potential for better marriages.

Marriage?

The fact that more and more people are questioning marriage as a viable alternative in itself increases the need for groups in which adolescents and even adults (especially those recently divorced) can engage in in-depth discussions of the advantages and disadvantages of marriage and other lifestyle decisions, including cooperative career planning. Even those who reject the idea of marriage usually realize that they still need close, intimate relationships with some person or persons for whom they care deeply, with whom they can share openly, and from whom they can sense genuine caring and wholesome emotional support. They, too, must be able to communicate what they are willing to give as well as what they expect to get from a relationship, and to develop a contract that, whether written or not, reflects both parties' agreement on issues that each feels are crucial to the relationship. However, many people who elect not to marry have difficulty developing clear understandings about their relationships with others. They often want for themselves the freedom that they are unwilling to give their partners.

Prior to marriage, people should devote thoughtful study to questions such as these: How can my close, intimate, loving relationship needs be met best? To what extent do I expect a prospective spouse of mine to become a genuine, participating member of my family, my extended family, and my circle of friends? Is this reasonable? How important are children in my life plans? Choosing between marriage and its alternatives is in itself difficult for some young people, especially when they are strongly influenced against marriage by their peers. Heretofore most such pressure was directed toward marriage and family, but today some youths are feeling even stronger peer pressure to live with an opposite-sex partner without marriage, to live with a same-sex partner, or to live in communes. Furthermore, they are reluctant to admit to friends what they really value and how they really feel about such living arrangements lest they be scoffed at by peers whom they really admire and whose respect they value highly. Group counseling helps such persons present their own real views, request assistance in

Is it all right for me to decide what is best for me and what will enhance my career?

coping with controlling friends and relatives, practice being more assertive, decide what is really best for themselves, and be more tolerant of others' views.

The Sources of Conflict and Pain

Some people allow themselves to be coerced into marriage. As many as one-third of first-born children are conceived out of wedlock, forcing many people into "shotgun" marriages (Otto, 1976). Others continue courtships in spite of doubts they have about the quality of the relationship because they do not want to hurt the prospective mate or because they lack the courage and interpersonal skills to break the relationship.

Other couples become bored with each other when they discover that they do not experience the continuing passion of new "love." They are reluctant to settle for anything less than a continuing passionate romance. They require assistance in learning to live in the real world:

> If they experience the joy of love (or imagine they do) for 10 percent of the time they are married, attempt to treat each other with as much courtesy as they do distinguished strangers, and attempt to make the marriage a workable affair—one where there are some practical advantages and satisfactions for each—the chances are that the marriage will endure longer and with more strength than the so-called love matches (Lederer & Jackson, 1968, p. 59).

So many people who have serious marriage problems have learned only how to attract others and to begin relationships. They are good hunters, but they lack maintenance skills. They require help to discover what they can genuinely respect (or learn to respect) about their mate, what they really like and enjoy about their mate, and what they must do in order to develop a good friendship with their mate.

But even becoming good friends is not sufficient. Most couples, especially people who are successfully married and do not feel threatened by divorce, sincerely want to enrich their relationships. They seek help in developing closer, more intimate relationships in order to become more genuine with each other, to learn to share joys and sorrows with each other, and to express tender, loving feelings for each other. Such couples also tend to be interested in improving their communications with each other—to make requests rather than demands and to detect early the signs of developing conflict and to cope with it. Those with troubled marriages require these, too, and usually they can be helped better in groups that include couples with good marriages who are committed to making them better.

The need for closeness and intimacy and the fear of it are common problems of those who seek marriage counseling. In order to experience closeness and intimacy, a person must believe that his mate understands and respects their differences and that closeness to his mate will not threaten his identity. When intimacy is not developed, the need for it tends to be replaced by anger and hostility, and each partner tends to feel undermined by the other (Papanek, 1971).

Closely associated with the unfulfilled need for intimacy is sexual dysfunctioning. Frequently, sexually dysfunctioning clients have not learned to accept their own sexual needs and/or adequacy. They also may perceive themselves and their mates as not being sufficiently attractive to be desired. Some people look upon their mates, even at the time of their

Why do I want something so much when I am afraid that I can never have it?

Why do I want something so much when I am afraid that I can never have it?

marriage, as only the most desirable from a group of barely acceptable people. In many such cases neither partner has learned to accept responsibility for his own satisfaction.

People who seek marriage counseling have experienced other problems. Lederer and Jackson (1968) describe several of these destructive behaviors and/or feelings. One or both feel that their marriage is fraught with so many hurtful behaviors that it can collapse anytime. Typically their problems and conflicts are left unresolved and essential decisions are not made. One or both partners fail to take the initiative required to determine their own behaviors and feel sorry for themselves. At least one plays "poor me" to achieve mastery, and one or both expect disaster even when things are going well. They play the "cross-complainer" game—responding to a complaint with a complaint—and one reacts to the other's differences as marks of inferiority rather than merely as differences.

To what extent have marriage problems changed in recent years? The following marriage problems commonly reported ten or fifteen years ago are reported today: lack of communication, unmet emotional needs, child-rearing problems, sexual dysfunctioning, money, in-laws, alcoholism, and physical abuse.

> Men and women in the 1970s probably have no more marital difficulties than they had in the 1940s and 1950s. The difference is couples today believe they have a right to feel better. Never before in the history of marital relations have so many husbands and wives believed that they were entitled not only to be free of boredom and suffering, but free to experience, on a fairly regular basis, satisfaction, joy, and even ecstasy. This feeling of possibilities concerning sexual and emotional satisfactions has created an unprecedented demand for feeling good (Koch & Koch, 1976, p. 20).

Three common new problems have to do with women's newly won equality: (1) the wife makes demands the husband feels unprepared to cope with; (2) both reject sex-role sterotyping but have not learned to give up old roles and to live new ones; and (3) both have difficulty in meeting the self-sacrificing demands of marriage and family.

In the early years of marriage, couples require much help in clarifying expectations, developing and revising marriage agreements (both implicit and explicit), learning new roles, and cooperating when making decisions. Whereas perhaps young couples require more help than ever before to cope with family responsibilities and to learn cooperative decision making, older couples still require assistance in freeing themselves from parenting responsibilities (Koch & Koch, 1976).

> While there are some young couples who want treatment out of a mutual recognition of danger signals and out of a joint desire for growth so as to get ready for children and/or to make life altogether more satisfying, the majority of young couples come for help because of severe clashes from the start of the marriage which threaten to produce a total breakdown. Unlike couples in latter stages of marital development, these younger couples, as a rule, are not yet really married except in the term's most external connotation. Their ties to their respective primary families are often extremely strong and one can rightly state that the couple plus their parents constitute the *de facto* family. Just as in later marital stages the children are the focus of the difficulties, in this early period of marriage parents and in-laws become objects of marital strife and hostile dependency (Gurman & Rice, 1975, p. 180).

Is Marriage Counseling Effective?

Although reviewers are critical of the research designed to appraise outcomes of marriage counseling (Gurman, 1973; Olson, 1976; Paquin, 1977), most agree that clients are helped by marriage counseling (Gurman, 1973; Olson, 1976). Olson reported that those counseled made significantly greater gains on over half the criterion measures than the control subjects (similar people who did not receive marriage counseling). Gurman reported a 90 percent success rate for the four best-designed studies he reviewed. Meltzoff and Kornreich's (1970) broad appraisal of counseling and psychotherapy also concluded that the success rate is highest for the most carefully designed studies that they reviewed.

Furthermore, researchers have reported some conclusions that are useful to practitioners. Their findings supported counseling husband and wife together in a group. Those obtaining marriage counseling on an individual basis had the highest divorce rate, while the best overall results were obtained by spouses counseled together, both in groups and by themselves (Olson, 1976). Gurman also concluded that there is no supporting evidence that the use of co-counselors produces a higher rate of success.

Nevertheless, researchers must continue to develop improved criterion measures that counselors as well as researchers can use to appraise clients' growth (e.g., the type of criteria that a counselor and client develop from the client's behavioral goals rather than general appraisal by personality tests), define more precisely their techniques in order for others to replicate their research, and describe the competencies of the counselors who provide the counseling. It is not sufficient for them to ask the general question: "Is counseling effective?" They must try to determine which techniques are most helpful or hurtful under what conditions, including what combination of clients. Researchers also should try to assess the impact of the techniques they use to select clients for counseling, to prepare them for counseling, and to appraise clients' commitment to learn and implement new behaviors.

Who profits from group counseling?

From a review of the research we also have learned some things that counselors can use to select clients more effectively, and thereby improve the chances for making the counseling more effective. Those who profit most from group counseling have been described as follows:

1. They seek assistance on their own. These people are easier to help than those coerced into counseling by friends and relatives (Beck, 1975; Johnson, 1963).
2. They discuss their problems openly, solicit feedback, accept feedback, and take the necessary risks to implement desired new behaviors (Lieberman, Yalom, & Miles, 1973).
3. They have a desire for growth, some flexibility, some capacity for insight, and some wholesome, early childhood experiences with authority figures (Stranahan, Schwartzman, & Atkins, 1957).

4. They are able to become ego-involved with others (Allport, 1960).
5. They are able to invest in helping others and reap satisfaction from observing others solve their problems (Ryan, 1958).
6. They are able to make an emotional investment in helping at least one other group member (Lindt, 1958).

Those who are likely to benefit most from counseling seem to have many of the same characteristics that differentiate a-chievers from nonachievers (McClelland, 1971):

1. They are challenged by opportunities for growth.
2. They are willing to work hard to achieve their goals.
3. They prefer to solve the problems for themselves rather than to rely on others.
4. They require precise goals and criteria to appraise their own growth.
5. They habitually think about how they can do things better.

There are some distinguishing characteristics of poor prospects for counseling outcomes. The last two are particularly relevant to marriage counseling:

1. They have difficulty making the commitment to attend every session (Spielberger, Weitz, & Denny, 1962).
2. They fail to discuss their problems openly and to become meaningfully involved early in the life of the group (Sethna & Harrington, 1971).
3. They are unable or unwilling to define precise behavioral goals for themselves (Ohlsen, 1977).
4. They have a strong need for revenge—to get even with their spouse (Ohlsen, 1977).
5. They are unmotivated to change and have a variety of other problems in addition to their marital problems (Paquin, 1977).

In other words, the best prospects for counseling come to counseling prepared to do what successful clients do in counseling groups and to learn their desired new behaviors. On the other hand, the poorest prospects must be helped to decide whether or not to contract for counseling; and if they elect to participate in counseling, they must be given extra assistance in order to prepare them to profit from it. Perhaps some will want to discuss whether or not marriage is a viable alternative for them.

Poor prospects for marriage

Poor marriage prospects doubt their ability to develop close, intimate relationships with opposite-sex partners; they question their ability to perform well with opposite-sex partners; they have not experienced healthy closeness and perhaps even fear it; and they have difficulty defining and communicating the essential conditions for a lasting relationship. They have difficulty negotiating a contract and accepting the responsibility for living by the guidelines defined in the contract. Even most of these people can learn to be effective marriage partners when they sense precisely what they would gain from it, when they decide precisely what they must learn, including completing unfinished business with those who have contributed or are contributing to their present state, and when they can make the essential commitments to learn and implement desired new behaviors. They can be counseled most effectively in mixed singles groups. However, it is crucial that they be screened with great care to ensure that they accept fully their responsibility for their own growth and that they demonstrate their commitment to learn new behaviors and implement them. Usually they can be treated most effectively in groups with at least some others who have real problems of their own but have experienced some close, intimate, heterosexual relationships and hence can serve as good models.

There are others for whom continuing marriage with their present partners does not seem to be feasible. They no longer look upon their spouses as persons with whom they want a close, intimate, continuing relationship. They have been hurt too much by past failures, or their need for revenge cannot be discharged or replaced. Their family lifestyles, their values, their religious beliefs, their ambitions, and their expectations from a marriage are too incompatible. However, even such persons can profit from counseling in couples' groups. They, too, can learn to listen to each other, to discover the peak experiences they have had together, to complete their unfinished business with each other, and to say wholesome goodbyes. They can help each other decide what each does not like about himself and what new behaviors each must learn to improve. They can review their failures and learn what they can do to prevent them in a new relationship—and even help each other determine the type of person with whom each would have best chances for a successful marriage in the future.* Thus, they can learn from their failure in marriage, minimize the scars of separation and divorce, begin looking back upon the parts of their past together with some happy recollections, and perceive their spouse as a friendly acquaintance rather than as an enemy.

Fortunately, most couples can be helped by marriage counseling. Whether or not this is achieved depends on the extent to which the couples presenting themselves for counseling are like those who are most apt to be helped, the care with which they are prepared for counseling, their commitment to learn their desired new behaviors, the combination of clients placed together, and the counselor's skills.

Marriage as a Viable Alternative

Everyone needs close, intimate, lasting relationships with persons for whom they care deeply, with whom they can share openly, and from whom they sense genuine caring. Persons who fail to achieve at least a modicum of the feelings that characterize such relationships tend to become discouraged and depressed. They suffer from loneliness, unsatisfied "skin hunger," and a loss of hope. One way this is reflected is in the suicide rate. For a three-year period, one study revealed that the suicide rate is lowest for married persons: (1) 21 per 100,000 for married white males compared with 80 for divorced, 76 for widowed, and 44 for single males; and (2) 7 for married white females, 19 for divorced, 13 for widowed, and 8 for single females (Landis, 1975).

When humans lose their hope for the future and/or a better world to come, they become so demoralized that they fail to reproduce themselves (Gilder, 1973). As startling as this statement might at first seem, Gilder makes some provocative observations regarding the American intelligentsia:

> Contrary to popular belief, many influential groups in this society are already failing to reproduce themselves, and the country as a whole is now at a level

---

*This is something that most divorced people do not learn, and consequently they repeat the same mistakes in other marriages.

approaching zero population growth. Any increase in
this trend would signify a serious national demoraliza-
tion.

In the most elemental sense, the sex drive is the
survival instinct: the primal tie to the future. When
people lose faith in themselves and their prospects,
they also lose their procreative energy. They commit
sexual suicide. They cannot bear the idea of "bringing
children into the world" (Gilder, pp. 7–8).

Gilder argues that the bond between man and woman is
important to the survival of the human community in the ways
that matter most:

Without a durable relationship with a woman, a
man's sexual life is a series of brief and temporary
exchanges, impelled by a desire to affirm his most
rudimentary masculinity. But with love, sex becomes
refined by selectivity, and other dimensions of personality are engaged and developed. The man himself is refined, and his sexuality becomes not a mere
impulse but a meaningful commitment in society, possibly to be fulfilled in the birth of specific children
legally and recognizably his. His sex life can be conceived and experienced as having specific long-term
importance like a woman's (p. 37).

The high divorce rate in this country does not mean that
most persons have given up on marriage. Instead it means that
increasing numbers of Americans refuse to be satisfied with a
mere survival level of relationship. When they fail to see hope
for a growing, meaningful relationship, they seek new ones.
Women, in particular, are increasingly seeking a true marital
partnership as evidenced in the sharing of home and child-
rearing responsibilities and the right to achieve self-actualizing
experiences outside as well as within the home:

A 1974 Virginia Slims-Roper Poll of 3,000 women and
1,000 men shows 96 percent of the respondents still
believing in marriage as the cornerstone of life. In
spite of the enormous publicity given to living together

without marriage, living alone, living in a com-
mune . . . only 4 percent of those questioned in the
Slims-Roper Poll would prefer those alternative lifestyles. In another poll conducted by the Chicago Tribune, 7,000 Midwestern women returned question-
naires: 70 percent of those responding chose marriage
as the ideal life-style. Both the Tribune and Roper polls
do suggest a changing view of marriage, one which
we would call a family-lib or partnership-style marriage (Koch & Koch, 1976, p. 203).

Thus, most Americans look upon marriage as their best
alternative for developing lasting, meaningful relationships,
but they refuse to settle for barely tolerable relationships. They
come into marriage with higher expectations for satisfying relationships than their own family models and human relations
skills enable them to achieve. Many need to learn essential
new skills, to copy selectively from their models, to review
together and to develop cooperatively compatible lifestyles
and, when necessary, to seek competent professional assistance. To the degree that marriage partners can identify their
problems, are willing to cooperate in solving them, and are
committed to achieving a successful relationship with their
present spouse, they will markedly increase their chances for
successful marriage.

Unfortunately, most couples have seen and experienced
the power struggles that occur between spouses and perhaps
have been warned against "giving in." They have been encouraged by friends and relatives to establish a power position
and have had it modeled for them. Thus, even when they
understand intellectually the need for a partnership, cooperative planning, cooperative recognition and management of
conflict, and reinforcement of their mate's desire for personal
growth, they have few models to copy in implementing these
new behaviors. However, each can readily recognize and
criticize the other's failures and thus requires understanding
and assistance in implementing new partnership relationships. Frequently, each partner also has difficulty admitting the
extent of his need for intimacy and closeness. All these, and
even the problems of discovering and implementing agreed-
upon new child-rearing techniques, can be best learned and

implemented in groups with other couples. This is highly relevant for everyone who seriously considers joining a counseling group. Seeing other couples struggle with similar problems and solve them somehow encourages members to discuss their own problems and helps them to develop the courage and self-confidence to implement their own desired new behaviors.

Marriage is a viable alternative, but today people are confronted with new and more challenging problems. They are deprived of cooperative work and extended family and do not know or have readily available models that can be used to help implement desired lifestyles. And people expect more of marriage relationships. People cannot afford to abandon marriage as an institution until a good replacement for it is found— and for most people a good replacement does not exist at this time. Thus, as most people recognize what the situation really is, even more will seek out marriage counseling, marriage enrichment weekends, and parent education programs. It is likely that schools and colleges will markedly increase their adult education and adult counseling programs to supplement the parent education and counseling services currently offered by churches and regional mental health centers.

Summary

Everyone needs close, intimate, lasting relationships with others for whom he cares deeply, with whom he can share openly, and from whom he can expect caring and quality support. Today most couples move frequently, meeting with new people with new and different expectations. They lack the stability of long tenure in their home community with extended family, and while they have high expectations for an intimate, satisfying relationship, they often lack the models and personal skills to define and implement desirable relationships. Yet they are still called upon to deal with most of the problems of earlier generations. Most want a close, intimate relationship, including a good sex life, but many also fear it and wonder if they can achieve it. Today couples probably do not have any more marriage problems than couples had thirty years ago, but more people are aware of the possibilities for richer relationships and will not settle for less.

Marriage counseling can be effective when it is provided under appropriate conditions by a competent counselor. Best results usually are obtained when couples are counseled together, preferably in groups. However, it is generally agreed that the research on the effectiveness of marriage counseling must be improved. The suggestions made can be implemented, and more reliable data can be obtained in the future.

In spite of all the questions raised about survival of marriage as we know it today, it does appear to be a viable alternative. If nothing else, it cannot be abandoned until a good replacement for it is found. In fact, most people still perceive it as the best way for achieving long-lasting, meaningful relationships. Nevertheless, deciding among marriage and its alternatives is a crucial decision with which many people require assistance. To be helped they must believe that they can openly discuss their values and priorities, decide what is best for them, and believe that they will be able to implement their lifestyle with the support of those whose love and acceptance they value most.

Questions to Think About

1. For whom is marriage counseling most appropriate?
2. How do the problems that today's teenagers face differ from those that their parents faced as teenagers?
3. Which of the problems faced by couples seeking marriage counseling is most upsetting to you? Why?
4. How do you feel about those recent social changes that most clearly influence marriage and family life? What has been the impact of these changes upon your lifestyle?
5. What primarily interpersonal skills do people who are committed to improving their marriages have? For which of these skills have their models' behavior influenced them negatively? From whom can they learn to copy selectively?
6. How do you react to the idea of selecting only the most treatable people for counseling? What are the advantages and disadvantages of such a principle? How do you feel about the criteria available to you for selecting clients?
7. For whom is marriage a viable alternative? How do they differ from those for whom it is not a good alternative?

References

Allport, G. W. *Personality and social encounter.* Boston: Beacon Press, 1960.

Beck, D. F. Research findings on the outcomes of marital counseling. *Social Casework,* 1975, *56,* 153–181.

Gilder, G. F. *Sexual suicide.* New York: Bantam Books, 1973.

Gurman, A. S. The effects and effectiveness of marital therapy: A review of outcome research. *Family Process,* 1973, *12,* 145–170.

Gurman, A. S., & Rice, D. G. *Couples in conflict.* New York: Jason Aronson, 1975.

Johnson, J. A. *Group therapy: A practical approach.* New York: McGraw-Hill, 1963.

Koch, J., & Koch, L. *The marriage savers.* New York: Coward, McCann & Geoghegan, 1976.

Landis, P. H. *Making the most of marriage.* Englewood Cliffs, N.J.: Prentice-Hall, 1975.

Lederer, W. J., & Jackson, D. D. *The mirages of marriage.* New York: W. W. Norton, 1968.

Lieberman, M. A., Yalom, I. D., & Miles, M. D. *Encounter groups: First facts.* New York: Basic Books, 1973.

Lindt, H. The nature of therapeutic interaction in patients in groups. *International Journal of Group Psychotherapy,* 1958, *8,* 55–69.

Masters, W. H., & Johnson, V. E. *The pleasure bond: A new look at sexuality and commitment.* Boston: Little, Brown, 1975.

McClelland, D. C. The urge to achieve. In D. A. Kalb, I. M. Rubin, & J. M. McIntyre (Eds.), *Organizational psychology: A book of readings.* Englewood Cliffs, N.J.: Prentice-Hall, 1971.

Meltzoff, J., & Kornreich, M. *Research in psychotherapy.* New York: Atherton Press, 1970.

Ohlsen, M. M. *Group counseling.* New York: Holt, Rinehart & Winston, 1977.

Olson, D. H. (Ed.). *Treating relationships.* Lake Mills, Ia.: Graphic Publishing, 1976.

Otto, H. A. *Marriage and family relations: New prospective programs.* Nashville, Tenn.: Abingdon Press, 1976.

Papanek, H. Group therapy with married couples. In H. E. Kaplan & B. J. Sadoch, *Psychotherapy*. Baltimore: Williams and Wilkins, 1971.

Paquin, M. J. The status of family and marital therapy outcomes: Methodological and substantive considerations. *Canadian Psychological Review*, 1977, *18*, 221–232.

Ryan, W. Capacity for mutual dependencies and involvement in group psychotherapy. *Dissertation Abstracts*, 1958, *19*, 1119.

Sethna, E. R., & Harrington, J. A. A study of patients who lapsed from group therapy. *British Journal of Psychiatry*, 1971, *119*, 59–69.

Spielberger, C. O., Weitz, H., & Denny, J. D. Group counseling and academic performance of anxious freshmen. *Journal of Counseling Psychology*, 1962, *9*, 195–204.

Stranahan, M. C., Schwartzman, C., & Atkins, E. Group treatment for emotionally disturbed and potentially delinquent boys and girls. *American Journal of Orthopsychiatry*, 1957, *27*, 518–527.

3

HELPING CLIENTS
GET READY FOR COUNSELING

When a couple presents themselves for marriage counseling, the counselor tries to help them briefly discuss what their problems are and whose cooperation each will require to solve them. The counselor listens and tries to detect precisely where each hurts and what self-defeating behaviors each must replace in order to function effectively as a marriage partner. From the beginning, the counselor tries to help each spouse discover and develop his or her own problem-solving resources, learn to use them more effectively, and take responsibility for his or her own growth and for helping the other grow. Each has learned undesirable behaviors and, consequently, can learn desired new behaviors that will make it possible to function more effectively.

The Group Presentation

The group presentation is a description of the counseling process for prospective clients. These presentations can be made anywhere, though community organizations such as church groups, adult education or parent education classes, and community mental health centers are typical. Besides explaining what happens in counseling and what will be expected of them as clients and as helpers, the counselor gives some examples of problems commonly discussed by clients (see Chapter 2), tells how clients are helped, and answers prospective clients' questions. In other words, the counselor tries to provide prospective clients with the information they need to decide whether or not to participate and, when they decide to participate, to accept responsibility for getting themselves ready for counseling and starting to formulate their own goals for counseling.

When a counselor conducts a group presentation, he tries to be very brief, watching for prospective clients' reactions and questions and trying to make it safe for them to ask their questions. It is very important for successful clients to work from an internal frame of reference rather than an external one. For example, a counselor may introduce the idea of a typical problem as follows:

> Perhaps it would help you to know what persons like yourselves discuss in marriage counseling. Those who profit most from counseling discuss what really worries and upsets them about themselves rather than complaining about their mates, in-laws, children, or neighbors. For example, one of my clients spoke as follows about her problem: "I like to lie close to my husband and be cuddled when I first wake up in the morning and just before I fall asleep at night. Lately, my husband has been going back to work frequently after supper and when he stays home he watches TV and comes to bed after I have fallen asleep. In the morning he allows barely enough time to get to work after the alarm goes off." Here is an example of a good helping response: "When you think about this, you really get depressed. You wonder what is wrong with you and you wonder how you could begin talking to him about the problem." In contrast here is a less helpful response: "You wonder what's wrong with your husband? Why doesn't he appreciate you like he should?"

After the counselor has used one problem to teach prospective clients to discuss their own pain in first person rather than to complain about their spouse, he merely lists common problems discussed in marriage counseling (see Chapter 2).

Throughout the presentation he encourages prospective clients to interrupt with comments and reactions, to share experiences they have had in counseling, parent education, and encounter groups, and to ask how group counseling for couples will differ from their other experiences. At this stage the counselor must try to ascertain precisely what previous treatment methods they may have experienced so that he can tell precisely how his methods are similar to and different from their other experiences. Usually someone asks some questions such as the following: Will we really be able to talk openly about our problems in front of others? How will these sessions differ from bull sessions with friends? How can I be certain that confidentiality will be maintained? What risks am I taking in joining a marriage counseling group? Is it truly necessary in order to get help to confess everything that I have done wrong? May we have individual counseling sessions between group sessions? Why do you prefer group counseling over individual counseling? How often will we meet, when, and for how long? What are your expectations on attendance?

Whenever the counselor concludes that prospective clients at a group presentation have had ample opportunity to obtain the answers to their questions, he distributes slips of paper asking whether or not they wish to join a counseling group. On this slip of paper each person checks one of these responses: (1) yes, definitely, (2) no, not interested, or (3) maybe. In addition to her name, everyone who checks yes or maybe is asked to provide the following information:

1. Preferred meeting times.
2. With whom would you like to be placed?
3. With whom would you prefer not to be placed?
4. Do you feel your spouse would be more or less interested in group counseling than you?
5. Address and telephone number.

Those who check yes are contacted first (and they have been told that). In the meantime there are usually some people who check maybe and later decide that they do want to join a group or at least have an intake interview. There are also others who cancel their intake interviews or decide during the interview not to proceed with group counseling at this time.

The Intake Interview

When a couple who has not heard a presentation comes to an intake interview, the counselor begins with a brief presentation. Then he encourages them to discuss briefly what they believe their major problems are and whose cooperation they believe they will require in order to implement desired new behaviors. Very soon, however, he shifts the focus of attention to discussion of each *one's own pain* and to relate each of the hurts to the identification of specific new behaviors that each would like to learn with the encouragement and assistance of his spouse. As the wife listens to her husband discuss his pain and struggle to define his own desired new behaviors, her need to criticize, get even, or put him down diminishes and her empathy increases. Consequently, each one's willingness to cooperate in learning new partnership behaviors, e.g., cooperative planning, budgeting, improved child-rearing practices, or conflict management, is increased.

After both have discussed their hurts, defined their goals for counseling, and defined criteria they can use to appraise their own progress, most couples are ready to define their goals as couples. Some, however, do not reach that point until after they have actually entered a group, experienced genuine acceptance in the group, and have achieved some of their own personal goals. Still others are willing to join a group in order to achieve their own personal goals and to learn from their spouses, but are unwilling to define their goals as a couple until they have definitely decided that they are committed to a successful marriage with each other.

For the reasons cited above, as well as others, the counselor usually meets first with the couple, each alone, and finally as a couple, during the intake interview. When she meets with each spouse alone, she gives each a chance to discuss any problems that he or she is reluctant to discuss in the presence of the other, to practice discussing these and other difficult problems, and to review the extent of commitment to a successful marriage with this spouse. Finally, the therapeutic triad (wife, husband, and counselor) meets again to share whatever information that they have decided to share, to decide on whether to participate, and, if so, what goals they can agree to work on as a couple.

Both partners are rarely committed to marriage counseling to the same degree. When, therefore, one partner only agrees reluctantly to participate (say, the husband), additional intake sessions with the couple may be required to help him to decide whether or not he can accept counseling and make the necessary commitments to profit from it. The counselor encourages the committed one to proceed on her own to get ready to join a group (and to emulate good client behavior) and asks the reluctant client to help the counselor help his spouse to proceed toward implementing her own new behaviors. The counselor also encourages her to try to convey her disappointment with his reluctance to participate and enlists her assistance in helping her spouse explore the consequences of his unwillingness to learn new behaviors. Sometimes the counselor can detect and reflect the reluctant client's reservations about wanting his marriage to succeed as well as his genuine interest in learning from the relationship. If so, the counselor can reflect these feelings and enlist his spouse's assistance in helping him discuss them. Often this reflection, which facilitates the development of necessary commitments for successful counseling, may be achieved with a response such as: [To the husband] "I am genuinely pleased that you are able to discuss these doubts and to learn from this relationship—to learn to be a better marriage partner with her and/or someone else. [To the wife] I also appreciate your helpfulness in detecting his pain and in helping him own it. [To both] Much as I am pleased with your genuine, honest discussion of your real feelings and the commitment that you have just made to help each other, I feel obligated to point out to you [the one who claims to prefer a divorce] that you are taking a risk in deciding to join our counseling group. As a consequence of this experience you may decide to build a good marriage and give up your secret wish for a divorce."

Sometimes the reluctant client will agree to try counseling

I really want this marriage to succeed. I will work hard to improve myself and hope that he notices my sincerity.

on a limited term, e.g., five sessions, and to decide on the basis of those experiences whether to continue. Usually the group is reluctant to admit such a client, but sometimes he can convince them to admit him on probation. Thus, he must convince them that he is worthy of their trust and is committed to fulfilling the purposes of the group. When this is done, the group must be encouraged to spell out exactly what criteria they will use at the end of the probation period to determine whether they will vote to admit him on a continuing basis. Nevertheless, there is a tendency for other members to favor the committed spouse. When the counselor notices that the reluctant client is hurt by such behavior, she tries to detect the hurt, reflect it, and help that client tell the group how they are hurting him and what he requires of them. As long as he is permitted to continue in the group, the counselor as well as other members must be committed to help him learn his own desired new behaviors. Furthermore, if they decide that he no longer deserves membership, they are obligated to help him discover what he has and has not yet learned and what resources outside the group can provide further help. Such considerate behavior at the outset often convinces even the reluctant client to make the necessary commitments for continuing membership and to present his case convincingly to other members.

In addition to giving clients a chance to ask their questions about what will be expected of them in group counseling, the counselor lets clients identify those significant others with whom they will want to share their goals and from whom they will want to solicit reinforcement for their successes in implementing their desired new behaviors. Thus, even before their first group session they learn to differentiate between therapeutic talk and social conversation. They learn to detect pain, to facilitate discussion of it, and to encourage implementation of new behaviors. In other words, prospective clients have a pretty good idea of what will be expected from them as clients and as helpers, what their responsibilities are for developing and maintaining therapeutic conditions, and how to change their working agreements before they decide to join a group. Nevertheless, during the course of treatment, there will be times when clients will not know what is expected of them or they will recognize the need for new guidelines. In an effective group, clients recognize such need for structuring and feel sufficiently secure to ask for clarification or to suggest new guidelines. Moreover, the counselor should feel free to describe the conditions within which she functions best but also be flexible enough to take cognizance of clients' requests insofar as their requests enable her to use her helping skills in an ethical way. Effective structuring facilitates the therapeutic process; overstructuring and unnecessary controls interfere with its success.

Selecting Clients

Why is it important for a counselor to select his clients with care? Doesn't everyone who feels she needs counseling have the right to it? It should be evident why the counselor takes such care to ensure truth in packaging, to communicate expectations, and to convey to clients their responsibility for getting themselves ready for counseling, for defining their own goals. Careful selection enhances clients' chances for successful outcomes, communicates the counselor's caring, and makes counseling more attractive and safe. The counselor must be cautious about including three types of people: those who may be hurt by counseling, those who may hurt others, and those who may interfere with others' growth.

Those who may be hurt are fragile. They have learned to act this way or may be unstable. Often they also are afraid to discuss their problems openly or are defensive and resistant to change. Other clients become annoyed with the unwilling clients who won't own and discuss their problems openly and, consequently, attack their defenses. Some clients, especially those who are fragile, are vulnerable to the counselor's use of confrontation and of interpretation (techniques that normally should be used rarely if at all). Some also can be hurt when the counselor puts pressure on them to take a particular role in a role-played scene or to implement some new behaviors between sessions.

Clients who may hurt others tend to be insensitive to others' pain or to express anger or revenge against a group member to whom the role of a significant other has been assigned (see Chapter 7). Sometimes this type of client takes advantage of another group member. Fortunately, this kind of client usually does not seek assistance, and when she does, she rarely is able to make the types of commitments described earlier. Also, when the counselor uses interpretation, probing, and confrontation, especially when this type of client is in a group, he not only runs the risk of hurting clients, he also encourages clients to use these techniques.

The type of client who interferes with others' growth tends to avoid open discussion of her own pain and block or divert others' discussion of pain (especially pain closely allied to her own pain), tries to settle for vague general goals, resists implementing new behaviors, and protects others against pressure to implement new behaviors. Usually the counselor can identify this type of client in the intake interview by her unwillingness to discuss her pain openly and her resistance to defining precise behavioral goals. She doubts that facing her own real pain, defining the new behaviors that she would like to learn, and implementing these behaviors would really improve things.

Some counselors, and perhaps some clients, are uncomfortable with the idea of the counselor functioning as a

gatekeeper. Although the counselor does ask each prospective client in the intake interview to convince himself as well as the counselor that he wants to participate and is ready to profit from counseling, he usually discusses the admission of each prospective client with at least one colleague and rarely refuses a client admission to a group. When the counselor notices a client doubts the personal value of counseling, the counselor reflects these doubts and then tries to help the doubting client and, possibly, his spouse to decide whether he is ready and committed to profit from counseling. In other words, this decision is a cooperative one. In fact, either during the group presentation or the intake interview the counselor tries to include information that early in the decision-making process will help prospective clients determine whether they are a good bet for success.

Failure to include sufficient information about who tends to profit most and least deprives a prospective client of needed data and also causes a counselor to run the risk of not regularly asking himself whether the treatment can be justified. Two other possible harmful side-effects of a counselor's failure to select good prospective clients were noted by Wattenburg (1953): (1) counselors had more failures and were discouraged by failures and (2) referrers tended to evaluate counselors on the basis of these poor treatment bets.

Structuring

This technique is used to define expectations during the presentation and to further clarify them during the intake interview and during the first few group sessions. In particular, the counselor watches for and reinforces good client and helper behaviors. She may even stop the recorder, rewind a particular section of the tape, and replay it in order to help clients hear and grasp the impact of a particularly good exchange. She also may do this to introduce and explain the advantages of particular helping techniques, e.g., reflection (see Chapter 1) or role playing (see Chapter 6). Whenever, however, clients appear uncertain about what is expected or feel a need for new guidelines, the counselor facilitates clarification of expectations and/or formulation of new group guidelines (norms). The counselor has a stake in these decisions, too. Usually she has already described the conditions under which she functions best in the presentations. If members suggest a guideline with which she feels uncomfortable or even perceives as unethical, she should say so. Rarely will a group try to force her to accept such a guideline, but if they do, she must decide whether she can in good conscience continue to serve them as their counselor.

From the first contact with the counselor and other group members, a client must feel free to ask any questions he may have about expectations. The better the counselor can describe the necessary and sufficient conditions, help clients express their doubts about these conditions, encourage them to participate in formulating guidelines, and help them to learn how to function effectively within the group, the greater are the chances that clients will be helped. By recognizing and reinforcing good client and helper behaviors from the very beginning, the counselor enhances clients' open discussion of their pain and their implementation of their desired new behaviors. The way in which a counselor participates and encourages clients to participate, especially during early sessions, markedly influences the degree to which the group develops into a therapeutic group. Words alone are not sufficient. The counselor must reinforce her words with behaviors that encourage the most therapeutic behaviors and discourage the ineffective and/or hurtful behaviors (Psathas, 1960).

Summary

From the first contact with the counseling process a client is taught to accept responsibility for learning to trust his counselor and other group members, to get himself ready for counseling, to learn client and helper behaviors, and to implement his own desired behaviors. The presentation is given to help him decide whether to participate, to help him get himself ready for counseling, and to clarify expectations. In addition to understanding what was said in the presentation, the intake interview is designed to help clients assess their own readiness for counseling, to help them formulate specific goals, and to help them define criteria that they can use to appraise their own progress in counseling. Finally, each client learns to clarify expectations and to develop the guidelines his group will need to develop and maintain a therapeutic climate within the group.

Questions to Think About

1. How could you use structuring to facilitate the development and maintenance of a therapeutic climate within a counseling group? How might it interfere with achieving these goals?
2. As a client, what, precisely, can you do to get yourself ready and to help your spouse to get ready for group counseling?
3. If you were thinking about joining a marriage counseling group, how would you react to the type of group presentation described in the text?
4. With what type of client would you feel most uncomfortable in your marriage counseling group? Why?
5. What type of person would you like most to have included in your marriage counseling group? Why?
6. What do you think of the client selection process as it is described in this chapter? How could it increase and/or decrease your readiness for marriage counseling?
7. In addition to the information described in this chapter, what would you as a prospective client like to know in order to decide whether to join a counseling group or not?
8. With what ethical problems is a counselor faced in selecting clients for a marriage counseling group?

References

Psathas, G. Phase, movement and equilibrium tendencies in interaction process in psychotherapy groups. *Sociometry*, 1960, *23*, 177–194.

Wattenburg, W. W. Who needs counseling? *Personnel and Guidance Journal*, 1953, *32*, 202–205.

4

HELPING CLIENTS DEFINE GOALS

Most couples who seek marriage counseling can learn rather quickly to discuss their problems openly and to define precise, personal, behavioral goals for themselves.* As both spouses struggle to discuss their own pain, to define their own individual goals, and to develop joint goals, they discover that they can enlist each other's assistance in facing pain, in formulating goals, and in implementing desired new behaviors. These experiences decrease the threat of marriage counseling and increase clients' hopes for learning desired new behaviors.

Formulating Goals

When clients learn from the group presentations what is expected from them in counseling, they come to the intake interview prepared to discuss their problems and to define counseling goals. The counselor listens empathetically and tries to decide when they have discussed their problems sufficiently to expose their pain and the natural consequences of doing nothing, to understand the forces at work in their lives, and to develop the will to learn alternative behaviors before he tries to help them define goals. From the first contact with a client, the counselor tries to help each spouse discuss his own pain, relate each pain to an idiosyncratic, behavioral goal, and, where appropriate, divide a goal into mini-goals and/or develop a hierarchy through which he can move a step at a time, and to accept responsibility for his growth and reinforce his spouse's growth.

---

*Admittedly some persons do request marriage counseling merely to be forgiven for giving up on their marriage and to be told that it cannot be saved, but most request assistance with the sincere hope that they will be able to learn to function more effectively as marriage partners.

When new therapeutic material (both the conscious and unconscious dimensions of felt pain) is uncovered during a group session, a client wants other clients as well as his counselor to listen very carefully and to allow him to discuss what really worries him. When he feels that they are pushing him into defining his goals too quickly, he tends to wonder whether they really care and whether they have learned enough about him to help him decide what he must learn. Like the counselor, other clients also must listen empathetically and help him develop idiosyncratic goals that stem from his own pain. On the other hand, the counselor must not permit the client to wallow needlessly in painful material or to cathart to such an extent that his pain is alleviated and the motivation to change is dissipated. When the counselor is uncertain about the proper balance, he is probably right to intervene. It is usually better to err in the direction of helping the client define goals which are related to the pain discussed to date than to permit him to lose any of his motivation to change. New goals can be developed later as new pain is uncovered.

How can I achieve my own goals
and still help her achieve her
separate identity and goals?

How can I convey caring and
still achieve some of my own
personal goals?

When clients or the counselors uncover new material during counseling, there is danger that the resulting goals may distract a client from his original goals. Yet others can be encouraged to develop reflections that not only expose the pain they detect, but also help the client discuss relevant goals for that new therapeutic material and permit the client to decide where the new goal fits within his own priorities. Thus, each client comes to realize that he can decide when he will work on such new goals. Though he knows that he must face his pain in order to achieve his goals and that sometimes he may have to solicit other clients' assistance when he is tempted to evade pain, the client recognizes that the group is a safe, non-threatening place in which he can reveal his pain because he makes his own decision about what to discuss and when to discuss it. Nevertheless, some clients may overreact to formulating new goals after group sessions have begun, possibly out of fear that they will be stripped of their defenses as they have experienced or seen others mistreated by friends and relatives. When this happens, the counselor reflects this fear, helps the client see what is expected—i.e., to face the pain involved in the new material—and to decide whether he will agree to work on that material now.

Let me finish this before I begin working on another.

In addition to achieving his own idiosyncratic goals, a client usually improves his understanding of who he is as an individual, a family member, a friend, and a citizen; what gives him greatest satisfaction in each of these various roles; how to recognize, express, manage, and enjoy his feelings; and how to recognize early symptoms that suggest conflict and to deal directly with the relevant facts and persons involved. He learns to accept himself and others more completely, to give and accept love, to develop and to maintain meaningful relationships, and to change those unsatisfactory facets of his life which he can change with reasonable effort. Gradually he masters the essential skills for solving his problems and for developing relationships with significant others. He realizes that he is becoming a responsible, growing person who can cope with life as it comes (that he is developing ego strength) and that he is becoming more like his wished-for self. These general goals are desirable, but more precise goals are required to enable clients to discover their own growth, to appraise counseling outcomes, and to help counselors determine whether to continue, terminate, or change a client's treatment.

Realistic Goals

Successful clients either come to counseling with the confidence that they can learn desired new behaviors or acquire such confidence as they discover the other clients' and the counselor's confidence in their ability to learn. It also is enhanced by the definition of realistic, behavioral goals (including mini-goals when they are required).

Based on his personal experiences and research in industry, E. A. Locke (1968) concluded: (1) hard goals produce better performance than easy goals; (2) specific hard goals result in better performance than the general admonition to do one's best; and (3) behavioral intentions influence behavior. Motivated workers like to be challenged; they set moderately difficult but achievable goals and work hard to achieve them (McClelland, 1971). These conclusions apply equally well to the development of goals in counseling situations.

A counselor can do several things to help most clients define achievable or realistic goals. As each defines her own goals, the counselor can help in developing specific criteria that can be used to appraise her progress in achieving that goal. Developing such criteria tends to diminish the likelihood of setting unrealistic goals. Furthermore, when she discusses her pain and shares her goals during the first group session, other clients also are able to help her discuss very difficult goals, examine what her odds are for achieving them, and determine whether she is committed to make the effort and take the risks required to achieve them. When appropriate, other clients also can be very helpful in assisting her to clarify and convert unrealistic goals into more achievable ones.

Sometimes a client also can be helped to accept a level of success that heretofore she may have perceived as failure (anything short of perfection is failure). Usually the counselor is most successful with such a client when he can detect an unrealistic goal during the intake interview and thus alert other group members to this need for perfection when the client first discusses her goals within the counseling group. For example, in a group Clara described what the counselor perceived, and he thought that a couple of clients perceived, to be a success. Hence, he responded to Clara as follows: "Then you did talk to your mother-in-law about why you do not want her to buy your son that used car, and you didn't get into a fight, but you still feel like a failure. Nevertheless, you didn't handle the situation as well as Jack seemed to handle a similar situation with his mother. Anything less than perfection is failure?"

This reflection enabled several group members, including Jack, to give positive feedback and to help Clara formulate more realistic criteria for evaluating her efforts to change—to cope better with this particular situation. Such an experience not only gives fellow clients opportunities to practice expressing positive feelings to each other, but it also encourages this particular client to attack similar problems and to accept achievement less than perfection as success.

Sometimes the counselor realizes that a client's goal only appears to be overwhelming. In other words, the client may need a different strategy; that is, by doing one of several things the client can make the goal become noticeably more achievable. The counselor can help the client see that certain strategies are needed such as: (1) identifying, developing, and practicing a prerequisite skill and/or mastering essential prerequisite knowledge; (2) breaking the large, difficult goal into mini-goals and/or a hierarchy of steps that can be achieved one at a time; and (3) enlisting the assistance of relevant others. Other clients also can learn to provide similar help. Furthermore, they can detect when the client gets stuck, reaches a plateau in her growth, or is tempted to give up on a goal that is reachable. They can help her identify significant others outside of the group who will give encouragement and reinforcement. Group discussions help clients get in touch with other valued goals and lifestyle decisions that have been neglected and may require attention. Such awareness encourages them to examine their priorities. Frequently, clients also learn to seek assistance from relevant others outside the group in redefining their goals and ordering their priorities.

There are many explanations for why people set unrealistic, impossible goals. Clients sometimes unconsciously develop unrealistic goals in order to experience failure and to reinforce inferiority feelings (Dreikurs, 1962). Another explanation is that the individual tries to compensate for feelings of worthlessness by setting unrealistically high goals (Bieliauskas, 1966). Probably both the depressed and those who possess inferiority feelings set unrealistically high goals (Schwartz, 1974). In any case, setting unrealistic goals tends to be a part of such clients' lifestyles and a factor that contributes to their misery. Their unrealistic aspirations probably are instilled at an early age by perfectionistic mothers, fathers, and teachers and probably mass media. Furthermore, these persons tend to use only the most successful persons they know as criterion models for appraising their own levels of success (Krumboltz & Thoresen, 1969). Although such extreme cases usually can be detected in the intake interview, and even then can be helped by previously described techniques, they are difficult to help. Usually the best results are achieved with them when they are placed in groups with at least one or two such clients whom they admire and who have achieved some success in overcoming this self-punishing and self-defeating behavior. Such models can detect the problem readily, share the pain of their own previous self-defeating behavior and its negative impact on their spouses and other family members, encourage spouses to elaborate the extent of that pain, and model desired new behaviors. Clients with these unrealistically high goals also can accept the forceful but considerate pressure of these converts. For all such clients, early detection of this need to be perfect is important in order for the counselor to help them define precise goals and meaningful criteria for evaluating growth and surfacing the tendency to set unrealistic goals. These enable the counselor to help such clients develop realistic goals early, to define their own goals, and to evaluate their own progress in terms of realistic criteria.

Impact of Behavioral Goals on Clients

Why are behavioral goals so important for clients? First, acceptance of behavioral goals helps clients accept the notion that they can learn new, productive behaviors to replace their inappropriate or unproductive or self-defeating ones. During counseling they discover that they are not crazy—that they do not have to change their basic personality, lose their identity, or change their basic lifestyles. Furthermore, they will not have their defenses torn away by an authoritarian leader, nor will the leader encourage authoritarian members to tear away their defenses. Each group member decides when he is ready to discuss his pain. Clients also realize that though openly discussing what is really worrisome and upsetting is painful, it will be bearable and is likely to result in replacing some ineffective old behaviors with new effective ones. Also, with such a clear understanding that each client decides for himself what new behaviors he must learn, he does not have to worry about loss of personal identity nor being forced by his spouse or fellow clients into becoming someone different from what he wants to be. Instead, he knows that the counselor and other clients will help him hear his spouse's requests for change, consider whether these goals are appropriate for him, share his goals for desired new behaviors, and enlist his spouse's assistance in implementing his own new behaviors. Thus, the use of behavioral goals shores up the client's confidence in himself and in the counseling process.

Because each client must make a considerable personal commitment to earn membership in the counseling group, clients are encouraged to "open up" more readily and are able to focus on their problems and the solutions to them more easily. Research on industrial production supports this view and the model described in this book. The commitments required by the counseling process seem to be congruent with Notz's findings (1975), which support intrinsic motivation over extrinsic rewards. Goals developed through intrinsic motivation also seem to avoid the struggle against external control and to enhance the cherished notion of having one's own desired new behaviors result from one's own decisions (de-Charms, 1968). The importance of developing precise, behavioral goals is supported by Steers and Porter's findings (1974), too. Specific goals enabled their research subjects to focus their attention and efforts upon improved task performance. A person's commitment to his goals may determine how readily he gives up when he meets with difficulty and whether he abandons his more difficult goals (Locke, 1968).

Impact of Behavioral Goals on the Counselor

Periodically every counselor is expected to appraise every client's growth. She must try to obtain the answers to questions such as, Which of his goals has this client achieved? For those goals for which no growth can be detected, are the goals and the criteria for evaluating them clear? Does he understand them? Has he lost his commitment to achieve them? Is something or somebody blocking his progress? For which of these unachieved goals has he discussed relevant therapeutic material? For which does he either require mini-goals or the definitions of new skills in order to implement the new behavior? Is he the type of person who cannot profit from this treatment method? Is he being hurt by it or by someone in the group? Should he be referred to someone else for different treatment?

Besides his own case notes, careful analysis of recordings of the sessions, and feedback from respected colleagues, the counselor should periodically solicit feedback from his clients concerning his techniques and each client's progress in achieving his goals. In order to obtain helpful feedback from clients, he should listen to at least parts of a recording of a session (and preferably a video recording) and request answers to questions such as, Did I detect where you were hurting and facilitate your discussions of it? Where was I especially helpful in this responsibility? Where did I fail? Have I taught you to do this for each other? Where and how was I most successful in encouraging you to try new behaviors? Where did I fail to do this? What did you like most about this session? What did you wish that I would have done differently?

Summary

Most counselors tend to accept general goals, such as increased acceptance of self. These are not sufficient. When a counselor helps his clients develop precise behavioral goals and relevant criteria for each of them, his clients tend to be less threatened by the treatment process, to become more committed to learning their own desired new behaviors, and to have their learning reinforced as they discover specific ways in which they are growing. Meaningful participation in the goal-defining process tends to sustain a client's efforts when the going gets tough or the client reaches a plateau and is tempted to give up (intrinsic motivation).

Specific goals are essential for counselors, too. Obviously, counselors who do systematic outcomes research must have precise, behavioral goals in order to define criteria that they can use to select and/or to develop criterion measures for appraising their clients' growth. Even practitioners who rarely do outcomes studies must determine whether their clients are making normal progress. Specific goals are essential in order to define criteria for this purpose, too.

Questions to Think About

1. If you are a client and suspect that a given goal is more your counselor's goal for you than your own real goal, how could you check this out? What difference does it make?
2. Why is it important for you as a counselor to help a client convert vague, general goals into specific goals before accepting him for a counseling group?
3. What does it usually mean when a client tries to avoid defining precise behavioral goals?
4. What may a counselor do to encourage clients to accept responsibility for defining their own real goals?
5. How can a counselor determine when a client has discussed a problem sufficiently to define a goal?
6. What problems does a counselor face in helping a client define criteria he can use to appraise his own growth?

7. If you were to join a marriage counseling group today, what would be your primary goals? Which of these would have to be broken up into mini-goals?

8. For which of your goals would you have greatest difficulty developing adequate criteria to evaluate your own growth? Why?

9. Think for a few minutes about your perception of the critical elements in a good life. Which of these critical elements have you come closest to achieving? For which are your perceptions of a good life and your daily life most incongruent? Develop precise behavioral goals for the latter.

10. What is the danger of encouraging the client to formulate goals too early? How can a counselor detect when a client is pushed into defining goals too quickly?

References

Bieliauskas, U. J. Shifting of the guilt feelings in the process of psychotherapy. In J. L. Moreno (Ed.), *The international handbook of group psychotherapy*. New York: Philosophical Library, 1966.

deCharms, R. *Personal causation: The internal determinants of behavior*. New York: Academic Press, 1968.

Dreikurs, R. *Fundamentals of Adlerian psychology*. Chicago: Alfred Adler Institute, 1962.

Krumboltz, J. D., & Thoresen, C. E. (Eds.) *Behavioral counseling: Cases and techniques*. New York: Holt, Rinehart and Winston, 1969.

Locke, E. A. Toward a theory of task motivations and incentives. *Organizational Behavior and Human Performance*, 1968, *8*, 157–189.

McClelland, D. C. That urge to achieve. In D. A. Kalb, I. M. Rubin, & J. M. McIntyre (Eds.), *Organizational psychology*. Englewood Cliffs, N.J.: Prentice-Hall, 1971.

Notz, W. W. Work motivation and the negative effects of extrinsic rewards. *American Psychologist*, 1975, *30*, 884–891.

Schwartz, J. L. Relationship between goal discrepancy and depression. *Journal of Consulting and Clinical Psychology*, 1974, *42*, 309.

Steers, R. M., & Porter, L. W. The role of task-goal attributes in employee performance. *Psychological Bulletin*, 1974, *81*, 434–452.

5

BEGINNING COUNSELING

As the hour approaches for a new group to start, the leader experiences excitement and hope, reexamines clients' problems and goals, reviews each client's strengths, and thinks about possible critical incidents and how he can manage them. Clients also experience excitement, hope, and apprehension, and they think about their pain, their goals, and the expectations for which they require clarification. It is at this stage that the counselor can use several techniques to respond best to the feelings within both the clients and himself. If he is successful in applying these techniques, he will have gone a long way toward ensuring the success of the group.

Getting Started

Usually the counselor arrives at the meeting room a few minutes early, arranges the chairs, checks the recording equipment,* greets clients as they arrive, and introduces them to each other.

Following the presentation and the intake interview, most clients tend to come to the first group counseling sessions prepared to discuss their worries and concerns openly and to share their goals with fellow clients. Those who experienced the greatest difficulty in discussing their real pain during the intake interview have often been readied for this first group session by an extra intake interview that prepares even a shy or reluctant client to speak first in the group and to discuss his most difficult problems. The counselor also helps prepare this client's

---

*During the intake interview the counselor has explained how he uses audio and video recordings to enable clients to listen to parts of a session in which a client deals with a problem and/or role plays a situation and to consult with a colleague on difficult parts of the tape.

spouse to encourage and reinforce him for discussing his painful material early.

Joe was a reluctant client. Although he had let his wife Mary down in many ways, he still cared for her. He also felt inferior to her. Following several recent crises Joe reluctantly agreed to join a counseling group with Mary. Except when drunk, he had great difficulty discussing personal matters in others' presence—especially in the presence of women. In particular, he was uncertain that he could discuss his drinking problem and his abuse of Mary. Nevertheless, during the second intake interview he agreed to speak first and to discuss both of these problems, and he explained to Mary how she could be encouraging and supportive. After everyone was seated and ready to begin, the counselor reiterated why she preferred to have clients discuss their primary pain and share their goals prior to having them ask their questions concerning expectations and operational guidelines. Nevertheless, a couple of questions were asked about confidentiality which she encouraged clients to answer. Their answers seemed to satisfy

I selected these couples with care, and I believe it will be a very good group, even though Joe may be a problem.

those asking the questions, and she added a couple points on how confidences are sometimes broken accidentally and how clients tend to be hurt by such accidents.

Then she turned to Joe and said, "Joe is scared, but nevertheless he agreed to discuss his problems first. Please listen very carefully to his discussion of his pain, encourage him to discuss it, reinforce him for doing it, and help him decide precisely what he must do to cope with it—what new behaviors he must start implementing today."

Joe said, "I am sort of at the end of my rope. You can see what I did to Mary. In spite of my drinking and my bad treatment of Mary, I have managed my business well, and perhaps many who know me as a businessman would be surprised to discover how miserably I have failed in my marriage. I am really afraid that Mary has just about had it with me and a lot of great guys really like her. I am afraid she will take up with one of them and leave me."

Both Mary and the counselor registered surprise at the last two statements. These were new data. When no one spoke for a few seconds, Joe looked to the counselor for approval. She said, "Great, you really did it. You also introduced some new data that surprised me—kind of threw me for a moment. You have been working on this material since our last interview."

Several other clients in addition to Mary reinforced his willingness to face his primary problems—even expressed their admiration for his doing so. Then, the counselor added, "Now you can admit to yourself that you really care for Mary, that you want to keep her, that you have a drinking problem, and you are willing to work on it. I guess you also were surprised that your fellow clients didn't scold or admonish you— that they seemed to suffer with you and that they are willing to help you learn essential new behaviors for coping with both problems. I also detected that perhaps they sensed that you don't feel like you are any longer an interesting lover for Mary. Perhaps you'd be willing to check that out with Mary and to begin doing something specific about that this week too."

Mary said, "When you're drunk, I am afraid of you. Lately, I have concluded that you no longer really cared about me— nor that you were even interested in me sexually. In spite of all that has happened, I still prefer you."

Another female client said, "But I get the feeling you don't know where to begin—or with what."

Several other clients chimed in with suggestions about what Joe could begin to do immediately and offered encouragement. The counselor suggested that they also help Mary explore how she could, with Joe's help, differentiate between nagging and putting Joe down and being encouraging and reinforcing. Joe decided on a couple of things with which to begin; then the counselor told the other group members how much time was left so the rest could at least share a few things with which they wanted to begin getting help and clarify expectations for the development of group norms.

Joe's case illustrates how taking that first step helps both the individual client and the group. By taking a chance, Joe was reinforced for discussing his pain openly, and as he did so, other group members learned to detect underlying pain, to reflect it back to the speaker, and to use reflections to relate Joe's pain to desired new behaviors. They learned to recognize similar pain within themselves and to own it. Within such an atmosphere, they could look forward to working simultaneously on their common problems. The cooperative feeling taught them to improve their communication skills by, for example, learning to differentiate between requests and demands, to check out perceptions—especially those obtained from nonverbal cues—to detect early signs of developing conflict, and to manage such situations successfully.

Communication

Frequently when a couple seeks marriage counseling, they are locked into a power struggle. The struggle to establish mastery, whether it concerns a particular decision or the relationship in general, blocks genuine communication. Neither person really listens to the other, never sincerely checking out the other's intent, requesting and using feedback, giving considerate feedback, or making requests instead of demands. Each listens only for flaws in the other's logic and devotes all of his energy to organizing what he will say when he "captures" the floor. Furthermore, neither one recognizes this disparity in their conduct, but other clients quickly learn to recognize it and to help such a couple cope with it.

The group can help an individual grasp what good communication is:

> Good communication means having the impact you intended to have, that is, intent equals impact. In other words, good communication between intimates is clear and precise. The speaker tries to clarify the intent of his message by stating exactly what he is thinking, wanting, or feeling. He does not assume the listener "knows" what is going on in his head; he tells the listener so that the listener doesn't have to guess or mind read. The good listener tries to make sure that the intent of the message is understood, and does not fill in the gaps with guesses as to what is going on in the speaker's mind. Both partners are trying to make sure that intent equals impact (Gottman, Notarius, Gonso, & Markman, 1976, pp. 1–2).

Congruence is essential for effective communication. It is the accurate matching of those feelings of which the individual is aware and those which he is experiencing (Rogers, 1961).

How can I say what I need to say clearly, and still not be distracted by her frown?

Keep still. Really try to hear what he is saying. Don't let yesterday's fight interfere.

MESSAGE

Rogers illustrated lack of congruence with the case of the man whose flushed face, angry tone of voice, shaking, and finger pointing clearly suggested anger while his words strongly denied it. If, therefore, the sender is to transmit a clear message, he must be congruent while he is sending his message, and if the receiver is to hear accurately what the sender intended, he must be congruent while he is receiving the message. Usually other clients detect lack of congruence, but some require assistance in providing feedback and in helping the client who is not experiencing congruence to cope with his lack of congruence.

Feedback is essential to help a client discover his blind spots and to recognize lack of congruence. An individual cannot recognize his own lack of congruence: he needs the perceptions of others. Through the group process an individual discovers how he appears to others and whether his behaviors are having the impact that he intended (Golembiewski, 1972).

> Effective feedback encourages a client to listen, to explore its implications for learning new behaviors, to define new behavioral goals, to clarify what was communicated, to react to the feedback, and to solicit further feedback with reference to new goals and proposed actions. . . .
>
> Its acceptance is also determined by the receiver's perception of the giver of the feedback, the setting in which it is given, and the emotional state of the receiver. . . .
>
> Clients profit most from feedback from others whom they trust and perceive as motivated to help them. The better the feedback giver accepts the receiver and the better the feedback giver has exhibited caring and support for him previously as well as at present, the more credible the receiver perceives his feedback. First with the members of their counseling group and then gradually with their significant others clients learn to request and to give feedback. They also learn to express their feelings when they first experience them rather than either miss the expression of a tender feeling when it can be best shared or try to ignore a growing conflict until angry, hurtful feelings burst forth (Ohlsen, 1977, pp. 75, 78, 79).

Coping With Conflict

Since clients discuss what really worries and upsets them, they are encouraged to face conflict and resolve it with relevant target persons. Furthermore, clients do come to care deeply about each other, experience transference, hold different values, and learn to give frank feedback, and as a result the conflict among members is not limited to conflicts between spouses. Even when such conflict occurs early in the life of the group and even when it seems to be a transference reaction, clients are helped to face and resolve their differences. In fact, the entire group is encouraged to help the clients involved with conflict to obtain the answers to questions such as, What is the problem as you perceive it? Do you feel that you have the essential skills to resolve it? If you don't possess the essential skills, which must you learn? Whose cooperation do you require to solve the problem? How may you enlist the cooperation of these relevant persons? Who will contact each of these necessary helpers? What crucial points should be made to win the cooperation of these persons in order to resolve the conflict? To what extent is the resolution of this particular problem a matter of differences in values, lifestyle, or perception of the problem rather than the need for mastery of new human relations skills? To what extent does this conflict reflect the need for revenge or control over one's spouse?

Frequently, role playing can be introduced at this point to help a client more accurately communicate what his unique situation is like and what he must learn to cope with this particular conflict (see Chapter 6). The use of role playing involves more members of the group and often uncovers similar problems in others. As a result, many times the role players are encouraged to use role playing in dealing with their problems, too. Thus, clients discover early in the life of their counseling group that they can develop the assertiveness required to deal with conflict and, though it may be difficult, to own and express negative feelings to relevant persons. In addition, they discover that they feel stronger and more adequate when they have confronted that person and genuinely tried to resolve their conflict. Moreover, each party in the conflict is encouraged to deal directly with similar problems outside the group, to share successes, and to learn from failures in the counseling group.

Confidentiality

Prior to the first counseling session most clients realize that they can talk about anybody or any topic with the expectation that confidences will be kept. They also should realize that their reason for talking is to face their pain and to decide what they are going to do about it rather than to seek sympathy and pity or to embarrass others or merely to gossip. Furthermore, when methods described earlier are followed, most clients have asked their own special questions about confidentiality and either have obtained satisfactory answers or realized that it is an issue that the group must decide early. Listed below are some guidelines commonly developed by marriage counseling groups:

1. Except for the discussions that spouses have with each other and/or the counselor, no one discusses outside the group anything discussed in the group.
2. When an individual or a couple feels the need for a special session between sessions, they arrange for it during a regular session and use the special session to get ready to deal with the problem in their group.
3. When a couple discusses what went on in their group, they make certain that they talk where they cannot be overheard by others, and they focus their attention on pain uncovered in the group, getting ready to face a problem in the group, doing homework, or implementing and reinforcing desired new behaviors rather than gossip about others' problems.
4. When clients have learned and implemented new behaviors, and feel good about their successes and wish to share these successes with nongroup members, they realize that they do not have to give the group credit for their successes. They have earned them.

A clear understanding by clients concerning what is expected of them in their counseling group, including knowing what is expected with reference to keeping confidences, increases the security of the counseling group. Beck (1958) identified a number of additional reasons why a counseling group enhances self-disclosure:

1. It is easier to learn from peers.
2. Untrained peers give uncensored, realistic responses to one's self-disclosures.

3. Peers' feedback is less threatening than professionals' responses.
4. Peers listen and offer helpful assistance.

Clients also discover that others have problems that, perhaps, are more serious than their own.

The counselor's reputation as a helper, a keeper of confidences, and a manager of threatening events facilitates the development of security within a counseling group. First of all, he tries to ensure that clear agreements have been developed concerning keeping confidences. Furthermore, when anyone raises questions concerning a member's keeping confidences, he helps the group discuss it openly and, if confidences have been broken, decide what they must do with the one who let them down and how to prevent such occurrences in the future. His prompt handling of such situations and any other threat to the security of the group (and the discretion he exhibits in doing so) significantly contributes to the members' security within their counseling group.

Clarifying Expectations

The counselor encourages clients to begin their first session with the discussion of their pain and their goals rather than the clarification of expectations. There are several reasons for doing so. First of all, clients come prepared to discuss their pain, and the discussion of expectations tends to decrease that readiness while self-disclosures by everyone in the group increase that readiness and get everyone in touch with guidelines that each member feels are necessary to enhance the therapeutic climate of the group. Most groups develop some agreements on confidentiality, how to schedule individual or couple's sessions between group sessions, number of group sessions, attendance policy, length of sessions, and starting time. Rather than allowing himself to get hooked into being manager, the counselor should help the group to decide on a starting time and to stick to it. For instance, some groups like to work according to a signal, such as beginning when the counselor sits and stopping when he stands.

Of course, clients benefit from a reasonably precise delineation of how to make the process work well, but equally important is the fact that members of an effective group must be able to recognize when the group is not functioning well, to diagnose the group's problems, and to develop plans for improving its efficiency (Bradford & Mial, 1963). They also must learn to cope with conflict among members.

A counselor must be wary that he does not assume too much responsibility for members or function too much of the time as the group's manager or teacher. Whereas it is important for the counselor to teach clients to be good clients and helpers, he also must begin at once to help clients reinforce one another's good client and helper behaviors rather than to establish himself as a teacher or manager or even as the only helper. Whenever the counselor notices, especially during the first few sessions, that a client is functioning well as a client or as a helper, he should reinforce this behavior by calling it to the attention of other clients. Some counselors who regularly make video recordings of their sessions stop the tape while they are reinforcing the behavior by talking, rewind the relevant section of the tape, and show the particular behavior just discussed to the entire group.

Primary structuring is done during the presentation and the intake interview. Further structuring occurs whenever clients are either uncertain about what is expected or sense the need for new guidelines and request them. Sometimes, however, they have understood and accepted an existing guideline but do not want to enforce it. For example in one group the members understood and accepted the rationale for not complaining about one's spouse. Furthermore, they had agreed to help a particular couple stop coping with complaints by countercomplaining, but when June complained about Jack's failure to notice and compliment her on the very successful party she gave for Jack's business associates and Jack started complaining about June's low-cut dress and flirtations with his boss, the group just groaned and did nothing.

In an effort to help the other clients get in touch with their responsibility, the counselor commented as follows: "You are really disgusted with June's complaining and Jack's response with a countercomplaint, but you appear unwilling to express your disappointment directly to them and to insist that both discuss what really worries or upsets them. Perhaps my intervention will enable you to express your real feelings to them and to review for them what you really expect them to do now.

What is each really worried about? What can you say to facilitate discussion of that pain?"

Then Barbara said, "Since they cannot seem to act like adults, perhaps we can use a signal to stop the discussion whenever either complain or countercomplain—maybe stand up and point at the violator. Are you as disgusted with them as I am?" The response was a resounding "Yes."

Barbara added, "Is my suggestion for shutting off their inappropriate behavior OK?" Again the response was a clear, loud "Yes."

Then Ralph said, "Perhaps by now you are willing to talk about how awful you feel, June, when he seems not to notice you or to need you; and you, Jack, can tell how frightened you are when she seeks out other men."

Ralph's response to Jack was correct, but it turned out that June was in fact trying to initiate a relationship with Jack's boss. In any case, Ralph's response helped both of them begin to talk about their own pain and to decide what they wanted to do about it.

Bringing the Session to a Close

A few minutes before the time is up for the session, some counselors summarize what happened and review each client's commitments for homework during the week. But usually this is not required. At the end of the first session the counselor may ask if anyone has additional questions about expectations or if anyone needs help deciding what to work on between sessions or needs to role play what he plans to do. At the beginning of the second session he reviews clients' expectations and their responsibilities for planning homework, developing the courage to do it, practicing those skills which are required to do it, and reporting on either their successes or their failures.

At the close of a session most members appreciate getting a signal that the session is over, e.g., the counselor stands up and says good-bye. Some clients will require assistance in saying good-bye, and others may have trouble thanking those who have been especially helpful or finishing unfinished business with others. These are skills that clients should learn during the course of the session, but if they don't learn them at that time, the closing can be used for this purpose.

Keeping Records

Client's log

Soon after the close of each session, each client is encouraged to record the highlights of the session for himself: important topics that he discussed, what he wished he would have discussed, feedback he wished he would have requested, the homework he agreed to do, who helped him most by doing what, and who hurt him most by doing what. Clients also are encouraged to keep a record of the topics that worry them between sessions, the new behaviors they would like to try, their dreams, and where they succeeded and failed in implementing new behaviors. A log is a convenient way to do this.

Counselor's log

Counselors also are encouraged to record relevant information about each group soon after its session: What were the highlights of the session? How does he feel about it? Who was helped most? Who was helped least or even hurt? Is there any client about whom the counselor is especially concerned? What new therapeutic material and/or goals were revealed? To whom did he make any special commitments? Again, a log is a convenient way of recording these feelings.

Between sessions some counselors record ideas that occur to them concerning individual clients' pain, what they think each client wants to do about it, and write reflections that may either facilitate discussion of pain or relate specific pain to desired new behaviors. During group sessions the counselor reviews his notes of each client's goals and records new understandings. As he listens, observes, and doodles, he often develops improved reflections which he can edit and easily use later, when appropriate.

Even those counselors who tape every session will have to develop some simple system for recording the highlights of sessions. Since it is impossible to take the time required to listen to the recording of each meeting, the counselor must develop a system that enables her to capture the salient points of every group meeting. Such a record provides the counselor with data that are essential for the appraisal of the impact of a session on individuals and the identification of new therapeutic materials; also this record provides the basic data needed for self-study, clients' feedback, and feedback from a colleague on a particular segment of the recorded session.

Summary

Taking the first step is, for most people, always the most difficult part of a new experience. This is certainly true for group counseling. After each client has had a chance to discuss some of his primary worries and concerns, the counselor helps members agree on group norms. These norms usually include agreements on self-disclosure, beginning and closing sessions, termination, keeping confidences, commitments to implement new behaviors, and attendance. By helping group members establish clear and reasonable agreements, the counselor facilitates success for everyone in the group.

Questions to Think About

1. What might you as a counselor do to encourage treatment within the group by the group rather than counseling one individual at a time in front of the others?
2. How may you as a counselor differentiate between therapeutic interactions and social conversation among members?
3. Why should the counselor emphasize the temporary nature of a counseling group?
4. How may the use of audio and video recordings in a group be justified?
5. How can reflections be used to help clients learn new behaviors?
6. Imagine that you are sitting in your office thinking about the clients you selected for your first marriage counseling group. What are your primary good feelings? What are your most scary feelings?
7. What problems do you expect to be concerned about as you think about your first counseling session? What can you do to minimize the negative consequences of these problems?
8. What would you say if one of your clients said, "I feel very uncomfortable about you recording our sessions"? How could preparing her for the use of recording increase the productivity of the session for her?

References

Beck, D. F. The dynamics of group psychotherapy as seen by a sociologist. *Sociometry*, 1958, *21*, 98–128, 180–197.

Bradford, L. P., & Mial, D. When is a group? *Educational Leadership*, 1963, *21*, 147–151.

Golembiewski, R. T. *Renewing organizations: The laboratory approach to planned change.* Itasca, Ill.: F. E. Peacock, 1972.

Gottman, J., Notarius, C., Gonso, J., & Markman, H. *A couple's guide to communication.* Champaign, Ill.: Research Press, 1976.

Ohlsen, M. M. *Group counseling.* New York: Holt, Rinehart and Winston, 1977.

Rogers, C. R. *On becoming a person.* Boston: Houghton Mifflin, 1961.

6

USE OF ROLE PLAYING
IN MARRIAGE COUNSELING

The professional literature tends to emphasize how role playing can help clients cope with negative feelings, but it is needed
even more to help clients in other areas of their lives. Marriage
counselors can use role playing to help a client communicate
her feelings more accurately, to discover unfinished business
with specific significant others, to negotiate for an acceptable
level of intimacy, and to practice the human relations skills
required to implement desired new behaviors. When a client
plays her spouse's role in order to achieve any of the purposes
presented above, she senses her husband's pain more fully
and accurately, discovers unfinished business that she had
never recognized before, tends to become more highly motivated to help him rather than to criticize him or complain about
his faults, and models new behaviors for her spouse.

On the other hand, while role playing is a powerful technique, it is not a panacea. The counselor should look upon role
playing as only one of many effective techniques in his professional arsenal. When clients are able to communicate well,
have mastered the interpersonal skills required to implement
their new behavior, and possess the self-confidence and commitment to implement them even at the risk of suffering some
pain, role playing usually is not needed to help clients achieve
their goals.

Role playing in marriage counseling groups tends to be
more successful when the counselor video tapes the session.
This procedure preserves the nonverbal as well as the verbal
responses for analysis following the role-played session. When
a client plays her own role, the other clients are able to help her
capture her view of herself, and when she plays her husband's
role, they help her discover how she perceives him. The group
helps her husband to discover his wife's perception of him and

his unfinished business with her, to see himself as others see him, and to obtain suggestions for improving his behavior.

But what happens when the primary client, the one who is discussing her problem and asking for help (the wife in the case described above), does not try to portray an adversary accurately? She may merely try to make him look bad and to win from the group sympathy for herself. For example, a mother may assume her son's role and portray him to be even more hateful than he actually ever has behaved. This rarely happens, but when it does, some clients in the group usually detect the unfair portrayal and confront the client. Frequently, the other clients also invite such a client to bring in the rest of her family for a family session just prior to the couple's session. Such a session provides the other clients with new data and gives them a chance to help her entire family.

Introducing Role Playing

During the group presentation the counselor usually describes a situation in which he has used role playing to help a couple identify and practice implementing new behaviors. This kind of example serves two functions: it shows how couples can practice new behaviors and how role playing is used. It also should be used during early group sessions. The following case is an example of this.

When, near the end of the first session, Kevin fumbled for words to express his concern about his wife's (Ruth's) lack of commitment to saving their marriage, the counselor said, "Maybe you will remember the example I used in my presentation to illustrate how you can use role playing to practice telling someone how you really feel. Perhaps one of the other women would be willing to play Ruth's part and help you get ready to tell Ruth how you really feel about her and what it would mean to you to have her discuss her own real pain and try to learn to become her new wished-for self. Hopefully she will even help you learn essential new behaviors for a good marriage."

Kevin said that he would like to try it but wondered whether he could really do it with Ruth observing. After he finally agreed to try, provided that Ruth would sit where he could not see her, and a female client (Celeste) volunteered for Ruth's role, the counselor suggested that they begin with roles reversed to prepare Celeste to take Ruth's role and to give Celeste a chance to demonstrate to Kevin how he could initiate the discussion. Except for a couple of questions that Celeste asked about Ruth's behavior, little discussion followed the role-played role reversal. They role played the scene again with Celeste in Ruth's role (and, conceivably, exaggerating Ruth's negative behavior somewhat). Immediately following the second role-played scene, Kevin asked Celeste for feedback and then turned to the rest of the group for feedback. Everyone except Ruth participated.

While the counselor was preparing the video tape for re-play of both scenes, Ruth began to cry. After she discussed her fear of seeing herself as she really is, she began discussing what she disliked about herself and what she wanted the group to help her with. The session ended before she was through. The group agreed to let Ruth talk first the next time and then to study the role-played scenes. Ruth also volunteered to try to listen to Kevin if he elected to discuss this situation with her before the next session. These agreements were followed up in the next session. Even though Ruth felt that she and Kevin had been quite successful with their homework, Kevin still insisted that they practice it again in front of the group and get their feedback. At first Ruth appeared to be a little embarrassed or angry, but both seemed to profit from the role playing and the feedback. Following that experience, Ruth seemed to be much more open and committed to working on her problems.

Following the discussion of the video tape and the practice session that Kevin requested, the counselor reviewed when role playing seems to be effective for such couples, described its essential components, and explained why any member should feel free to request it for himself or another client. The counselor added that if the one suggesting it does not request it for himself, the one for whom it was recommended should have the right to accept or reject the suggestion.

Guidelines

Whenever the primary client (the one who requests practice of a scene for himself) accepts the idea of using role playing, he serves as director. He describes the situation to be enacted, does the staging and casting, and prepares the actors for their roles. Usually actors and any agreed-upon auxiliary "egos" are selected by the director from among the volunteers. Even reticent clients who rarely participate in group interaction will often volunteer for roles that are difficult but personally relevant to their own situation. Before the role playing begins, the primary client (director) discovers much new information about the situation, the characters in it, and himself from describing it, casting, staging, and preparing actors for their parts. If roles are left unfilled, the counselor encourages clients to suggest persons for these roles. Though he keeps his participation to a minimum, the counselor uses reflections to help the director communicate the appropriate feelings harbored by the characters and to help any clients who are having trouble expressing their characters' feelings.

Basically this is an impromptu play. After the players have been briefed and each has had a chance to clarify his role, each actor should feel free to express his character's feelings spontaneously. Even though each may have been given his character's words, he should try to get in touch with his real feelings during the real scene and to concentrate on expressing his character's feelings as he interacts with the primary client rather than trying to remember his character's precise words.

During the role playing the counselor also should teach each actor to use soliloquy to express her character's genuine feelings whenever she believes the character is experiencing incongruence and thus says one thing and feels another. For example, at one point while Celeste was playing Ruth's role, she paused, obviously editing what she said. At that point the counselor intervened and commented:

> You appear to be experiencing incongruence. You seem to want to say, "I wish you'd be straight with me, look at me, and share your real hurt," but instead you said, "I wish that we could enjoy one another's company more." From now on, when you feel that way, say to the target person what you feel comfortable saying and then cup your hand to the side of your mouth and say to the rest of us what you'd really like to say. This is soliloquy. Using it will help you detect your lack of congruence, communicate the hidden message to the rest of us, and enlist our encouragement in

helping you to learn to talk straight. The use of alter ego also can be used to help you do this. Whenever any one of us feels that you aren't acting congruently, we will stand behind you, put our hands on your shoulders, and interrupt the interaction to say for you what you may have said in soliloquy had you recognized your lack of congruence.

Just before using role playing for the first time or two, the counselor should check that clients understand role-playing guidelines and that actors are prepared to play their roles. During the role playing every actor should realize that he is free to use his own words to communicate his character's feelings and needs and to stop the interactions when he needs additional information on the role or is expected to do something he feels uncomfortable doing or saying. Usually the primary client stops the role playing when he has obtained the assistance he wants, when he wants to clarify the interaction of the characters, or when he wants feedback on what has occurred. After the primary client has a chance to obtain sufficient feedback, the counselor helps each actor shed his role (de-role) and assume his own real self in the group. For clients who have trouble getting out of their assumed roles or have trouble allowing others to give up their assumed roles, some counselors use a ceremony in which players formally move out of the setting in which the role playing was done, pretend to take off their assumed role masks, and return to their old seats in the group circle as themselves.

The primary client gains most from the role-played scene because it focuses on his problems. Moreover, he is helped to review what he learned about himself, his problem situation, and the feedback.

Other role players also reap special benefits from experiencing another's pain. They become aware of their own unfinished business, discover how significant others feel—empathize with them, get in touch with significant others' feelings toward them, and learn from peers' feedback. Those who benefit least are the observers or audience. When, however, the counselor encourages observers to participate by providing feedback and assuming alter ego roles when they feel that they can enrich the therapeutic interaction, they feel more meaningfully involved, too. Even an observer has the opportunity to encounter his real self and his problems and to experience some real joy in assisting his peers.

Even if the director does a very good job of describing the various roles, it is usually advisable for him to reverse his role, playing the part of his love object or adversary. Role reversal enables the director to clarify the message to be presented, to receive feedback on it and how it may be presented, and to get in touch with some of his own hidden messages as he prepares a volunteer for his role. A careful critique of the role-played scene provides him with feedback on a model's behavior. The playing and critiquing of his performance in his significant other's role gives him a new view of himself as well as increased empathy with his significant other. The use of role reversal also prepares the volunteer to play the crucial role in the scene.

The rest of this chapter is devoted to describing several role-playing techniques that many counselors have found useful in couples groups. These techniques are especially useful in helping clients get in touch with their own feelings, sense their own problems, and empathize with others.

Celeste, do you realize what I really want to say to Ruth? I'll be fair and I hope Ruth will be fair to me.

Techniques for Revealing Positive Feelings

One frequent problem of many clients is detecting positive feelings and actually expressing them to their spouse. Belinda's case is an illustration of how life rehearsal enables clients to do this.

Belinda had taken the day off work to do some shopping. Soon after she returned home, she had a call from Fred, who suggested that they go out for dinner. Although they did this frequently, she felt especially good about it this time. That night they went to the place where they had gone on their first date, yet all the while she failed to express the joy she felt, even though she recalled the benefits of doing so from their experiences at their marriage enrichment weekend retreat.

The next night she shared her feelings with her counseling group and asked them to help her express the depth of her good feelings. She wanted to say more than "Thanks, that was great." At first Fred said, "I know how much she enjoyed it"; then he admitted that he wished she could learn to express these warm, wonderful feelings—in both words and actions. Before Belinda practiced what she really wished she could express, she discussed her great need for intimacy and fear of it—her fear that once these feelings were expressed, the object of her affection might not reciprocate and she would be left with egg on her face. She also documented how she had been let down and expressed deep concern about whether her marriage to Fred would last—whether she was capable of developing and maintaining a close relationship with any man. Then she asked Fred to observe while she practiced telling a volunteer what the dinner date meant to her. After she received feedback on it, the group urged her to practice telling her role-playing partner what her marriage to Fred meant to her, where she felt they had failed, and what she required of him to own and enjoy intimacy and to enhance their chances for a good marriage. When she did that, they asked her to practice these statements with Fred. She was more cautious with Fred, but she expressed herself well and received some excellent feedback from him. Because of her caution, the counselor encouraged her to continue to work on expressing her feelings.

Human Potential Laboratory materials can be used very effectively in conjunction with life rehearsal exercises (Mc-

Holland, 1968; Otto, 1970). Adlerian counselors use early recollections to help clients in group therapy to get in touch with
goals pertaining to safety, security, self-esteem, and success
and to protect them from insecurity, danger, and frustration
(Papanek, 1972). Some counselors also use recollection of early
memories to help clients identify persons with whom they have
unfinished positive business: "Relax and close your eyes and
think about some specific unexpressed positive feelings. For
whom do you have these warm, positive feelings which have
not been expressed? What do you wish that you could have said
to each of them? With whom in this group would you like to begin
to practice expressing these unexpressed, positive feelings?"

Gestalt relaxation and fantasy techniques also can be
used to help clients to get in touch with their feelings and
concerns. Clients are taught to relax, to fantasize, and to recall
and report dreams that reveal their unfinished business with
specific persons (Polster & Polster, 1973). One way to report
these fantasies in a counseling group is to say the following:
"You know how to relax and how to get in touch with a dream or
a reoccurring fantasy. Open your eyes, select a peer from
among the volunteers, tell him whose role he is to play, and
share the unexpressed or inadequately expressed positive feelings with which you just now got in touch." As usual, when
group members have had a chance to think about and evaluate their experiences, the counselor helps the client prepare to
follow through to apply his practiced skills with the significant
other outside the group.

Techniques for Managing Intimacy

Magic shop
Magic shop is a self-presentation exercise which is used to
help a client to uncover his problems and to define goals (Carpenter & Sandberg, 1973; Shaffer & Galinsky, 1974). The client
is invited to present himself to the Magic Shop, in which his
spouse or a role-playing substitute is the proprietor, and barter,
not for merchandise, but for desired new personal characteristics, relationships, or behaviors. For example, in Fred's case
(see p. 75), the counselor could have used this technique to help
Fred barter with Belinda for improved direct communication of
positive feelings. When a client does this with a role-playing

partner first, he also is encouraged to practice making requests and defending his priority of requests with his spouse.

Breaking in
Schutz (1967) describes *breaking in* as a technique that can be used to help a client who is experiencing alienation, isolation, or loneliness:

> The people identified as "in" stand and form a tight circle with interlocking arms. They may face either inward or outward depending upon whether the person trying to break in sees them as simply involved with each other and ignoring him (face in), or as deliberately attempting to keep him out (face out). The outsider then tries to break through into the circle in whatever way he can, and the group members try to keep him out (p. 131).

After the primary client either breaks in or gives up, the counselor encourages group members to help the primary client evaluate what happened by asking questions such as, "How do you feel about what happened? Of what did this experience remind you? What did his behavior convey to the rest of you? What did each of you learn about him? What would you encourage him to work on with whom?"

Approach-avoidance
Schutz recommends another exercise, called approach-avoidance or the encounter. He describes it as follows:

> How: the two persons involved are asked to stand at opposite ends of the room. They are instructed to remain silent, look into each other's eyes, and walk very slowly toward each other. Without planning anything, when the two people get close to each other, they are to do whatever they are impelled from within themselves to do. They are to continue the encounter for as long as they wish. After it is completed the principals will ordinarily talk about their feelings, and the others will contribute their observations and identifications with the principals. It is essential to urge the principals to try to let their feelings take over and not plan what they will do when they meet.

Caution: there are no special problems with this experience. It can be revealing and unsettling, but people usually know whether or not they are ready for it.

Example: George had just been divorced and appeared to have much hostility as well as great attraction toward women. His feelings about women were apparently very confused, but he treated the whole area flippantly and with many jokes. Marla was very attractive and had very ambivalent feelings toward men. She was very dependent on them on the one hand, and very competitive on the other. She and George had avoided each other in the group until someone remarked their feelings toward the opposite sex seemed similar and wondered how they felt about each other. Characteristically neither could identify or verbalize how they actually felt toward the other. They said that they didn't feel anything. It seemed like an appropriate time for an encounter since it might allow them to become aware of their feelings toward each other that were being blocked inside them. They approached each other slowly and when they met, George looked at Marla briefly and walked right by her, staring straight ahead. For fully five minutes both stood still, backs to each other, looking in opposite directions. The tensions became too great for the observers and they began to urge the principals on to various resolutions of the impasse, but George and Marla accepted none. Then Marla stepped back, took George by the shoulders and turned him around so that she was facing his back. She then stepped back and the group waited anxiously for the next move. They didn't have to wait long, for Marla stepped up and delivered a tremendous kick in the rear of George, knocking him several feet across the room. Stunned, George just looked at Marla, who invited him to kick her back. He refused until she finally took a pillow and put it behind her. Reluctantly, George kicked her, but gently.

The effect of this interchange was different for the two participants. Marla felt elated and strong, her participation increased, and she became softer. Later in the psychodrama, she was able to work on her relations to her father, which helped her clarify her feelings toward men. George became depressed. His difficulties with women were serious and he was forced to face them directly, something he had successfully avoided up to that time (pp. 141–142).

In this instance, the technique was especially useful for Marla. It also helped other members understand George's real pain and perhaps enabled them to help him admit to his pain and to decide what he was willing to do about it.

When using this technique, some counselors encourage clients to use soliloquy to reveal their feelings and wished-for behaviors, and even to solicit suggestions from other group members on how to cope with their situation. Frequently, this approach enables clients to openly discuss feelings that they have been trying to get up the courage to discuss. It also can be used with singles groups to encourage open discussion of the need for intimacy and the development of dating skills.

All humans have a need for intimacy. Learning to touch appropriately and expressively is essential for learning to be intimate. Otto (1971) makes the case for clients' need to touch as follows:

> The thought and word are not our primary mode of communication. We are primarily animals who touch!

That George could be very nice. I wish I could tell him that without appearing pushy.

I wonder what she is really like. How can I tell whether she is soft and loving or hard and pushy?

> Our deepest thoughts and feelings can only be com-
> municated by touch—by physical intimacy. . . .
>   We can become more aware of our bodies not
> only through loving, caring touch, but as a result of
> certain exercises and experiences. . . . Most of these
> exercises and experiences have been used for some
> time by Human Potentialities classes sponsored by
> various colleges and universities, and participants re-
> port excellent results (pp. 36–37).

In Chapter 9 several cases are presented to illustrate the use of intimacy exercises to practice communication of specific requests and the development of intimacy skills. Such role-playing exercises help clients who need greater intimacy to recognize their real needs and express them to relevant persons. These exercises also help them negotiate the amount of intimacy they can accept and endure.

Clients can also use their own experiences and the excellent ideas and case materials presented by Bach and Deutsch (1970) to develop scripts for role-playing scenes.

Conflict Management: Top Dog–Underdog

Many couples' conflicts develop out of a power struggle (Chapter 11). Each tries to control the other. The Top-Dog–Underdog technique (Polster & Polster, 1973), which Gestalt therapists use to help an individual discover and learn to manage the internal conflict between master and slave within herself, can be readily adapted for use with couples in group counseling. Role playing can be used to help them identify which spouse is usually master and which is usually slave. In the discussion which follows the role playing, the counselor and clients listen, try to detect and reflect the unique pain of slave and master, help each to define relevant goals, use role playing to practice desired new behaviors, and decide which behaviors to work on as homework.

Nancy had always managed finances and Jim, a police patrolman, seemed to appreciate her good management. When she went to work, a power struggle surfaced, and it got much worse when she became a partner in a very successful business. After a short separation they joined a counseling group. Early in the second session the counselor described the Top Dog–Underdog technique and asked Nancy and Jim to identify instances in which each was slave and master. The other clients concluded that Jim was usually slave and Nancy was usually master. The counselor sat Nancy in a large comfortable chair and Jim in a small uncomfortable chair. He asked them to tell how they felt in their roles and helped them identify issues for which control created conflict. Then he asked them to role play a recent incident in which they had a power struggle, to reverse roles, and to reenact the scene in their top dog and underdog roles to show how they managed this conflict. It was only at this point, when she sat in Jim's underdog chair and suffered in his role, that Nancy was able to grasp the depth of Jim's pain. This experience motivated her to define and try some specific new partnership behaviors and to give up some of her belittling putdowns. Furthermore, the other members rallied around Jim and encouraged him to try some specific new assertive behaviors in order to present his needs more effectively. Until the top dog grasps what he is doing to the underdog and the underdog discovers how he uses "poor-me" behavior to get what he wants at a big personal loss in self-respect, neither is motivated to change. Nancy and Jim's growth also was enhanced by the many areas in which they were functioning well.

Cooperative Decision Making: Fiddler Game

When Tevye in "Fiddler on the Roof" analyzed a problem, he would present the argument for a decision and follow with "On the other hand," and present a case for the opposing position. This technique has been used effectively to help a dependent client in individual counseling, and it can be used to teach a couple to do cooperative decision making too.

To prepare a couple to use this technique, the counselor describes how it works and explains why it is effective. First the group helps them decide for which of the two choices for a particular decision each believes that he or she can make the best case. Then the counselor says "On the other hand," and each make his or her case for the other choice.

Rebecca, for example, complained frequently about her

in-laws' meddling, in particular about her mother-in-law's pressure on them to have a child. Eventually, she and Mark felt that they had to decide now whether or not to have children. Since they were somewhat uncertain about whether or not they could agree, they decided to write their own independent analysis of the issue. Using the Fiddler Game, both agreed to begin with the argument, "I want to have children" (leaving open the decision on number and timing for a later time), and to list both pro and con arguments in the order of their importance. After much discussion they finally agreed to spontaneously list all the pro arguments first, then the con arguments, and then order each list in a priority after much private thought and review. Each did this with the understanding that they would share both lists with the group after first role playing their spontaneous responses in the group.

Interestingly enough, they agreed on pros and cons better than they anticipated. Furthermore, to everyone's surprise, they made both decisions at once. They decided to have two children and to start soon. Both seemed pleased with their cooperative planning and with the assertive but considerate procedures they had developed for coping with Mark's meddling parents. The fact that another group member noted how they had learned to function as partners, instead of being divided and conquered by his parents, reinforced their behaviors. Following that observation, the counselor asked whether there also were other people who either Rebecca or Mark let control their lives. The discussion that followed further generalized their new learnings.

Summary

When clients can discuss their pain openly, define new behaviors, and implement them, they can learn new behaviors that will help them cope. They don't need role playing. But many people can't do this. For them, role-playing techniques can be very helpful.

Role-playing techniques are used in marriage counseling to facilitate a client's discussion of his pain, to surface problems of which he is not aware or is reluctant to admit, to increase sensitivity to his own and his spouse's real feelings, to practice completing his unfinished business with relevant persons, and to practice partnership skills. Role playing enables a client to improve communication with group members, to accept and apply feedback, and to see himself as others see him. Thus, role-playing techniques are very valuable adjuncts to marriage counseling in groups.

Clients should be introduced to the use of role-playing techniques as a part of the treatment process during the presentation and be taught to use them in one of the early group sessions. When the counselor detects a good situation for which a client can use role playing, he should explain how to use it for that particular situation. After it has been used successfully in the group, the counselor can explain how members can identify those problems and people for whom it is appropriate. Furthermore, in addition to helping members learn to describe the problem situation, select the cast, and prepare each to play his role, it is important to teach clients to disengage themselves from their role-played roles and to return to the groups as themselves.

Seven techniques were described in this chapter. Each of them has a particular use in specific situations, but all of them, if used properly, can help clients define their pain, identify desired new behaviors, and implement them.

Questions to Think About

1. What are the pros and cons a client should consider when deciding whether to accept a role when role playing is used in a counseling group?
2. How may role playing be used to cope with transference in a counseling group? How may it be used to manage resistance in a counseling group?
3. How may the primary client gain advantages from critiquing that section of a session in which he used role playing to deal with his problems?
4. How can soliloquy be used productively in a marriage counseling group?
5. Select the three role-playing techniques you feel that you could use most readily. Describe what the unique advantages of each would be for a marriage counseling group for which you were the counselor.
6. During the intake interview the counselor learns that Marvin

wants but fears intimacy, even with his wife. Early in the second session Martha describes her need for intimacy and her husband's fear of it. Following considerable discussion of her pain and her husband's encouragement to experiment with new approaches, she decides to try the approach-avoidance exercise. Without realizing the extent of Marvin's fear of such intimacy, she asks him to role play it with her. If none of the clients try to help Marvin deal with this threat, what will you (as counselor) do to help Marvin respond to the request and, if he agrees to participate, to prepare for the role-played scene? Both Marvin and Martha are attractive persons and may even be attracted to each other.

References

Bach, G. R., & Deutsch, R. M. *Pairing: How to achieve genuine intimacy*. New York: Avon, 1970.

Carpenter, P., & Sandberg, S. The things inside: Psychodrama with delinquent adolescents. *Psychotherapy: Research and Practice*, 1973, *10*, 245–247.

McHolland, J. D. From stress to release of human potential. Speech. Evanston, Ill.: Kendall College, 1968.

Otto, H. A. *Group methods to actualize human potential*. Los Angeles: Holistic Press, 1970.

————. *More joy in your marriage*. New York: Pocket Books, 1971.

Papanek, H. The use of early recollections in psychotherapy. *Journal of Individual Psychology*, 1972, *23*, 169–176.

Polster, E., & Polster, M. *Gestalt therapy integrated: Contours of theory and practice*. New York: Brunner/Mazel, 1973.

Schutz, W. C. *Joy: Expanding human awareness*. New York: Grove, 1967.

Shaffer, J. B. P., & Galinsky, M. D. *Models of group therapy and sensitivity training*. Englewood Cliffs, N.J.: Prentice-Hall, 1974.

7

TRANSFERENCE AND COUNTERTRANSFERENCE

Whenever a client overresponds to another as if she is a significant other with whom he has unfinished business, he is experiencing transference. Usually he is not conscious of this process, but he can recognize what he is doing when it is called to his attention. This significant other might be anyone with whom the client has unfinished business from the present or the past, no matter how distant. He may harbor affection that he feels he has not expressed adequately; he may have failed to say his good-byes to an important person; he may have let a relationship languish that he now realizes means much to him and want to revive it; he may recognize unresolved hurt still exists between him and another; or he may want to resolve a conflict with someone who is important to him.

Thus, discussion of transferences can help clients identify unfinished business with specific significant others with whom they are currently having problems as well as problems carried over from early childhood. For example, Gail obviously liked Oscar from the time they were introduced during the very first session. Later in the first session, the counselor said to Gail, "You really like Oscar, don't you?" Reluctantly, and somewhat sheepishly, she admitted it. This comment stimulated a discussion of Gail's embarrassment over such affectionate feelings for men other than her husband, the threat such feelings aroused in her, her desire to learn to manage them better, and considerable group interest in learning to enjoy and manage opposite-sex friendships. When Gail spontaneously responded so warmly to Oscar, he liked it but felt uncomfortable. Before labeling Gail's transference feelings and helping her complete her unfinished business with the relevant significant other, the counselor used a life rehearsal exercise (similar to the one used by Belinda and Fred in Chapter 6) to help Oscar and Gail express and accept their feelings for each other and to discover that such feelings can be managed.

When the group started to shift to another topic without dealing with Gail's transference feelings for Oscar, the counselor said,

> Although this discussion really seemed to help you, Gail, and Doug [Gail's husband] was very helpful, your reactions to Oscar suggest unfinished business with someone. Very likely Oscar reminds you of someone for whom you have positive feelings but have never expressed them adequately or someone you have left behind without saying the proper good-byes. Unknowingly you have put his mask on Oscar and treated him as that other person. Perhaps you would be willing to discuss the unfinished business that you have with the person of whom Oscar reminds you and what you must do to complete that business.

What Gail did occurs in daily life outside groups too. Under the right conditions everyone is inclined to assign someone the role of a significant other and to relate to him as though he is that person. Even with positive transference, the transference object tends to feel uncomfortable because he has not earned the love and affection he is receiving.

Oscar is really nice. I could like him a lot, but I shouldn't.

I wish I could tell Oscar that I really like him.

Moreover, most persons tend to try to fulfill the roles assigned to them, both in counseling groups and in daily living. In
counseling groups they can be taught to recognize when transference occurs, to accept it as an indication of another client's
need to discuss their relationship, and eventually to help the
person who is experiencing transference to deal with the
source of the transference.

A Psychoanalytic View of Transference

Freud was one of the first therapists to recognize that though
transference can be an impediment to the development of the
therapeutic process, it can be useful, too. In traditional psycho-
analysis the therapist evokes projection and transference. He
tries to be a blank screen on which the patient is encouraged to
project and thereby become the all-powerful expert who uses
interpretations of the transference as the central theme of treatment: "As the patient repeats his infantile relationships in his
relationship to the analyst, his buried feelings emerge and
become accessible to interpretation. The repetition of the infantile conflicts under controlled analytic conditions enables the
maturing ego to reevaluate and handle more objectively the
early repressed conflicts" (Glatzer, 1965, p. 167).

Glatzer contends that deeply neurotic patients are unable
to love tenderly because their unconscious fantasies are so
centered around the oedipal and preoedipal figures that they
feel guilty about these fantasies and that their transference
objects are both loved and feared. Further, she believes that
transference within a therapy group is not confined to the
analyst and the analytic hour. It occurs during interaction with
other patients as well as with others outside their therapeutic
group. Within an effective therapeutic group patients learn to
give and accept mature love.

For Fried (1965) psychoanalytic group psychotherapy
stresses helping the patient experiencing transference to
recognize the unsuitability of emotions transferred indis-
criminately and automatically onto persons who do not war-
rant them. She also stresses the importance of helping patients
understand and learn to express more appropriately the feelings being transferred rather than focusing on the object of the
unfinished business:

While it is often vividly clear and amusing to see how, given the cast of a therapy group, a person will focus on a certain member as though he were, say, a domineering intolerant older sibling, and it is tempting to point this out, such recognition of transference object is of lesser value than understanding of the transferred emotions and defenses against them. If someone discovers that he falsely equates an older woman in the group with his mother, he will find this interesting, but, in and of itself, such insight will not prompt new reactions and actions inside or outside the group. It is more important that the patient find out what emotions he transfers to the transference objects and what defenses and adaptations he uses in dealing with these emotions. And, above all, the patient must genuinely discover that both the old emotions and the defenses and adaptations can be replaced by truly up-to-date reactions. This last step is the one that clears the road for new behavior (p. 50).

In a later paper Fried (1971) explains how the therapist elicits transference by remaining neutral and by presenting himself as a silent screen. When, however, the therapist's behavior can be observed more openly in a group, he is not as apt to evoke and sustain transference neurosis. Transference feelings tend to be interrupted or fragmented due to others' interruptions. Fellow clients also learn to convey effectively that those experiencing transference neurosis do not have to stay stuck in their uncomfortable ruts—that they can learn essential new behaviors to improve their ways of living.

In both papers Fried communicates clearly the point that most other analysts fail to stress: patients must be helped to learn essential new behaviors to function better in the present.

From his research, his clinical experience, and his study of group dynamics with Kurt Lewin, Bach (1957) concludes that much of what appears to be transference may be a reaction to reality. The transference object (the person being treated as the client's significant other) may look like and even behave somewhat like the client's significant other. Bach believes that clients' interactions may appear to be so appropriate that it is difficult for even an experienced therapist to distinguish between transference and justified reactions to what may be transference objects. When, for example, a female counselor or a female client responds warmly and empathically to a shy, naive male who is seeking closeness and intimacy from a cold wife, he is apt to perceive the helper's response as a love response rather than as the helping one that is intended.

Bach perceives transference as the individual's expression of unfulfilled regressive needs. However, clients do not limit themselves to reexperiencing early childhood experiences. Clients' interactions are so vivid and realistic that it is difficult for the person who is the transference object to avoid helping a client experiencing transference from expressing unfulfilled needs or unfinished business. Bach notes that, unlike dealing with the therapist in individual therapy, clients react when they are bombarded with transference. With the assistance of the counselor and other clients, the one experiencing transference discovers why people want to be loved or rejected for what they are and for what they have done rather than for what they appear to be. Thus, Bach involves his patients in the helping process more and perhaps places less emphasis on the psychologist's insights than classic psychoanalysts.

Why Does the Counselor Elicit Transference?

The degree to which a counselor elicits transference is determined largely by what he does as well as says in response to these questions:

- Does he believe that his clients have learned to be what they are—that they have learned some productive behaviors that should be reinforced and some self-defeating behaviors that must be replaced with more productive ones?
- What does he do to ensure that clients know what is expected from them before they decide to join a counseling group?
- What does he do to encourage them to take responsibility for their own growth, for helping to develop a therapeutic climate within the group, and for coping with their own resistance to change?
- Does he believe that most of his clients can discuss their real pain openly, can define desired new behaviors, are motivated to learn these new behaviors, and can define precise criteria which they can use to appraise their own growth?
- What does he do to ensure that a client's goals are truly the

client's own goals rather than someone else's goals for him?
- Does he encourage his clients to discuss early childhood experiences in detail?
- Does he seem to need to impress his clients with insightful interpretations?
- Does he believe that most clients must understand why they behave and feel as they do before they can improve their adjustment?
- Do his clients seem to be dependent on him?
- Does he encourage clients to use himself and other clients as transference objects?
- When a client exhibits transference, does he encourage her to discuss her relationship problems with the transference object and resolve their problems before helping her learn to manage these transferred feelings with the relevant significant other outside the group?

A counselor's confidence in his clients' ability to solve their own problems, his lifestyle, his professional preparation, his need to be an expert or the central or controlling figure in the group, and his feelings concerning fostering independence or dependence influence the extent to which he fosters transference in his group.

The counselor is never a completely blank screen. At least one or two people in the group detect his own feelings, values, needs, ambitions, pain, and hopes for them. Where he sits, how he behaves, and how he reacts nonverbally as well as verbally conveys a lot about him. In many communities and treatment settings clients also have a chance to get to know the counselor as a person outside of counseling. All of these circumstances can be used productively, provided that the counselor can communicate what he believes to be unique about the counseling relationship and how this intimate, trusting, temporary relationship can be used by clients to implement new behaviors.

On the other hand, even a group- or client-centered counselor is someone special in the group. His words and actions tend to be valued more than those of other members. Yalom (1975) describes the potency of the counselor's role in the group as follows:

Every patient, to a great or lesser degree, perceives the therapist incorrectly because of transference distortions. Few are conflict-free in their attitudes toward such issues as parental authority, dependency, God, autonomy, and rebellion—all of which often come to be personified in the person of the therapist. . . .

As a result of transference the therapy group may grant the leader superhuman powers. His words are given more weight and imbued with more wisdom than they possess. . . .Groups, including groups of professional therapists, overestimate his presence and knowledge. They believe that there are great calculated depths to each of his interviews, that he predicts and controls all the events of the group. Even when he confesses puzzlement or ignorance, that, too, is regarded as part of his technique, deliberately intended to have a particular effect in the group (pp. 195, 198–199).

Thus, while the roles that the counselor plays and the degree to which he accepts responsibility for clients can make clients dependent on him and help determine the degree to which clients use him as a transference object, he exerts a strong influence over clients even when he tries to avoid doing so:

The leader looms very large in the emotional life of the group. Try as he will he cannot shirk all the irrationally based trappings of his role. . . . Interviews with learners indicated that the leader's support and acceptance was of considerable value for some individuals in helping them to increase their evaluation of self-worth. Other members, through their constructive interaction with the leader, were able to reevaluate and to alter their relationships with parents or parental surrogates. Others identified strongly with the leader's world view and modus operandi; for example, even months later they might deal with a personal dilemma by trying to remember how the leader would have considered or handled a similar situation.

Conversely, strong criticism, negative judgment or rejection by the leader was received by some members as an exceedingly important indictment. Recall that the majority of the Casualties reported having been deeply affected by an attack or rejection by the leader. Some of the Casualties recalled months later some of the negative statements of the leaders with extraordinary vividness (Lieberman, Yalom, & Miles, 1973, p. 436).

Consequently, every counselor must be sensitive not only to transference but also to his own personal impact on clients. Peer supervision by a respected colleague of video tapes also is essential to help a counselor identify his productive and unproductive behaviors and the way he copes with his own projections onto clients (countertransference), and to improve his management of himself and the other therapeutic and antitherapeutic forces within the counseling group.

Developing Clients' Responsibility for Their Own Growth

Naturally, many clients feel dependent when they seek counseling. When the counselor and her services are not known to clients and the counselor provides little or no structuring, she elicits transference. To the degree that she continues to be a blank screen she encourages transference responses. Clients often find it easier to discuss their personal history and to have an expert explain how certain crucial elements in their lives may have shaped their behavior than it is to discuss where they hurt now and to decide what they must do to improve their own adjustment. In fact, when many couples begin marriage counseling, they know what their problems are and what they could do to resolve them, but often each spouse is waiting for the other to make the crucial, difficult changes and, perhaps, doubts his own ability to change or lacks the courage or the interpersonal skills required to change. Moreover, at least one spouse often fears that exhibiting willingness to change will be met with even more demands for him to change.

When, however, each spouse listens to the other discuss his pain, define desired new behaviors, and demonstrate the commitments required for membership in a couples' group, and discovers within the group a supportive climate for personal growth, he is genuinely encouraged to make the necessary changes. He then usually begins with behaviors that are relatively easy for him to implement. But after he has made the first step and has implemented some essential behaviors, he may confront a difficult problem that seems to halt his and his spouse's growth. Oftentimes such a person is inclined to give up. At this point the group members may support and even pressure him to continue to grow, express their confidence in his ability to grow, assist him in breaking down desired new behaviors in a hierarchy of steps or mini-goals, and offer their assistance in practicing new skills.

Before a client ever decides to join the kind of couples' group described in this book, he realizes what responsibilities he must accept for his own and other clients' growth. When, however, a client feels dependent or experiences transference with another group member, his counselor and other group members may be tempted to explain why he is experiencing transference. Instead of interpreting the transference, it is more productive to try to detect precisely how he feels, make an educated guess (a reflection) that will encourage him to discuss his real feelings, and subsequently to formulate a reflection that will tie his pain to new behaviors that will alleviate that pain.

In the counseling group a client is encouraged to express his real feelings toward his transference object. After he has expressed these feelings and solicited feedback from others, especially the transference object, the counselor may help the client relate his feelings to the relevant person outside the group with a comment such as "And is there someone outside the group with whom you have a similar problem, Karen?" If such a comment is sufficient, then the counselor merely goes on to determine whether Karen needs to role play the new behavior with her transference object before implementing it with the relevant person outside the group.

Usually, once a client has resolved a problem with her transference object, a short reflection is sufficient to help her generalize her experience to the relevant significant other outside the group. Sometimes, however, as indicated at the beginning of this chapter with Gail, the counselor uses a relatively brief interpretation to help the client identify the unfinished business she must complete and to decide whether she must practice the desired new behavior with her transference object before implementing it. Such a response conveys empathy, caring, and encouragement to make decisions for herself, and to accept responsibility for implementing those decisions. When followed by further reflections that relate specific pains to specific goals, the counselor's response facilitates learning specific new behaviors and discourages dwelling on the past. Even when the counselor's interpretation of a client's transference focuses on the transferred feelings, clients may intellectualize. However, for some clients interpretation of their behavior is highly threatening and increases their tendency to avoid the pain uncovered by interpretation of their transference. A few even feel that they have been attacked, and possibly their chances for becoming hurt have been increased. Moreover, use of interpretation tends to enhance the counselor's status, to make the client more dependent, and to cause the client to expect and want a prescription for coping with the person for whom he has unfinished business. Thus, if possible, the counselor should use reflection rather than interpretation.

Dependency

A dependent client usually has had his dependent behaviors reinforced by someone who needed to have someone dependent upon her. Moreover, such a client requires opportunities to learn and to practice independent behaviors and to be reinforced for acting independently. Frequently, he also must be taught new assertive behaviors. Helping such a client to identify specific decisions which he must make and to use the Fiddler Game to resolve such decisions also can be very effective (see Chapter 6). Some clients require instruction that can be obtained in a special session for the couple. Within the group, such a dependent client also can be helped best by another group member who is trying to learn to cope with a dependent significant other. As the first client listens to this client express her negative feelings toward her dependent significant other and helps her tell how angry she gets when she feels absorbed and used, he begins to wonder if that is the way his friends and relatives feel toward him. Until such a dependent client discovers the anger and hate experienced by those who feel used by him, discusses his relationships with valued friends who have deserted him, and recognizes his own need for self-respect, he usually is unwilling to learn the behaviors required for independence.

Acting out

When a client responds spontaneously and irresponsibly toward another, he is acting out. Such a client tends to feel that it is appropriate during therapy for him to express himself spontaneously without regard for others. Later, he often tries to justify his behavior on the grounds that his inhibitions were released by his counseling group and that, consequently, he could not be expected to act responsibly and exhibit his usual consideration (whether it is for the supervisor whom he struck or for the shy, naive client he seduced).

Some critics of group counseling and group psychotherapy genuinely question whether such acting out either can be prevented or used therapeutically within a group. In any case, eliciting transference and interpreting it tends to encourage acting out. Nevertheless, even those who use these techniques usually should be able to detect when clients are apt to act out and to prevent it by exposing a client's need to act out before it happens.

In most cases acting out is a form of resistance. Ziferstein and Grotjahn (1957) describe a type of patient who avoids facing his real pain and trying to learn essential new behaviors by acting out:

> As long as this deep oral longing is not understood, interpreted, worked through, and integrated, it will lead to acting out. It would appear, then, that not only in the case of acting-out characters, but also in the case of acting out in the course of therapy, the basic cause of acting is the patient's repressed orality, and that acting out is essentially a defensive maneuver against orality. . . .
>
> Acting out is a form of activity whereby a patient unconsciously discharges repressed, warded-off impulses and relieves inner tension. Instead of remembering certain traumatic and therefore repressed experiences, the patient relives them. However, the patient is unaware of this fact, and to him his actions seem appropriate to his present situation. . . .
>
> There are people in whom the tendency to act out is prominent throughout life. There are the "acting-out" characters, who are frequently found to be oral individuals, with low tolerance for frustration or postponement of gratification, and with defects in superego and ego formulation. . . .
>
> Acting out is only a temporary, and not a satis-

factory, solution. This analytic handling of acting out, as of any resistance, is prompt interpretation. With the help of interpretation, "acting out" is changed into "working through."

Acting out may involve the patient in realistic troubles, sometimes of a serious nature. This may complicate the treatment if the therapist reacts with anxiety and tries to restrain the patient by exercising his authority rather than by understanding and interpreting. The patient may then take advantage of the therapist's anxiety and punish him by further acting out, or he may react as to a forbidding parent with castration fear or submissive compliance. The result may be a chaotic situation, aggravated in part by the countertransference of the therapist and the other group members. Most important: the therapist and the group may vicariously enjoy the patient's acting out and unconsciously encourage him, perhaps rationalizing it with the idea that it's good for the patient to develop the courage to gratify impulses, test reality, learn in the school of life, etc. etc. In this situation the therapist and the group members are behaving like parents of delinquent children (Johnson & Szurek, 1952) who unwittingly encourage their children to act out the parents' own repressed impulses (pp. 81–83).

Acting out tends to be an expression of resistance—a substitute for the client remembering the pain, discussing it, and deciding precisely what he must do to cope with a particular problem. It also may be expressed as transference.

Even reasonably healthy persons try to justify their unacceptable behavior on these grounds. For example, as Betty described an attractive male co-worker (Albert) with whom she was going to a national convention, she unknowingly revealed her desire to seduce him at the convention. She seemed to be developing a case for using Albert as a guinea pig as she discussed application of her new assertive behaviors with males. The other clients picked it up and seemed to be enjoying it vicariously (and, to complicate matters, Betty's husband was absent at that session). The counselor struggled with a choice: Should he expose her plans to act out, and certain members' reinforcement of it, or deal later with the problem that would result from her acting out? He decided to express her need to act out with the following reflection: "You are pretty excited about having an affair with Albert at your convention, and some of the rest of you are enjoying her anticipated fun vicariously." Betty was embarrassed and responded angrily. The counselor in turn, responded: "You act angry but my guess is that you are embarrassed too. Perhaps now you even feel a little guilty, but maybe you'd feel even worse after you had your fling with Albert or he rejected your proposition." One of the group members owned his own excitement about her acting out and hearing about it after Betty returned from the convention. This well-timed reflection (the first sentence) exposed both Betty's and several other group members' motivations for their various behaviors and facilitated discussion of their own individual problems. No longer did they snicker when Betty talked about Albert. Neither did they condone or reject her desire to act out. They did convey clearly that she must decide for herself what she really wanted to do and accept full responsibility for her own behavior rather than to pretend that she stumbled into a situation she was not prepared to handle. Obviously it is better to prevent acting out whenever possible because, although it does point up problem areas and important concerns, it also may result in pain that could have been avoided.

In another case Clarence told the group about his wife's unreasonably aggressive behavior when she got drunk and the counselor failed to respond to Clarence's hint that he would beat up his wife the next time she did it. Unfortunately, most of the other members seemed to encourage him to react to her drunkenness. Worse still, his wife seemed unaffected by his ever so thinly veiled threat—even chuckled about it. In this instance the counselor was reluctant to use a reflection to expose Clarence's potential for acting out, probably wondering whether he had sufficient data for such a reflection. Consequently, Clarence did beat up his wife the next time she got abusive while drinking.

All were shocked when they saw her the next week. Clarence had beaten her up badly, and was embarrassed and rather frightened by his uninhibited response. Though Clarence's behavior was destructive and irrational, the counselor used his obvious pain to discuss, first, his fears and shame and then to decide what new behaviors he needed to learn to manage these acting-out tendencies. The counselor also helped Clarence discuss his genuine affection for his wife, the specific ways in which she had hurt him, and what he required of her. This helped her discuss her pain and her commitment to learn desired new behaviors to help herself and improve their relationship. During the discussion the group also uncovered a lot of Clarence's pent-up, unexpressed anger towards women, especially female authority figures, and helped him identify the persons with whom he had unfinished business and where he could begin to complete it.

Of course Clarence might have rejected a reflection similar to that which Betty's counselor made to prevent her acting out. If, however, Clarence would have accepted the tendency to act out exposed by a reflection, he could have been encouraged to discuss various other alternative actions for coping with his belligerent wife, to select one, and to use role playing to implement it with her. Possibly his preparation of the group for a role-played scene in which he expressed the depth of his shame and anger would have been sufficient in itself to warn his wife and to alert him to his real potential for acting out. Had they first reversed their roles to demonstrate what usually happened when she got drunk, it would have been very revealing to the group, and especially to his wife, to see how Clarence perceived her drunken behavior. If she had been well-prepared to play her role empathically (perceiving their relationship through her eyes), it could have been revealing for him to discover her perceptions of their problem too. Thus, his underlying motivation for acting out could have surfaced and been used therapeutically without the pain that resulted.

Perhaps acting out cannot always be prevented, but the counselor should recognize when it is apt to happen and teach clients to recognize and prevent it. It also is important to help the client who acts out to recognize when he is inclined to act out, to discover other means for expressing these needs, and to examine the consequences of irresponsible behavior. Usually a well-timed reflection can be used to uncover the need to act out and to enlist other clients' assistance in helping cope with it rather than condoning it. It also can be used to help both the perpetrator and the victim to express their feelings during a role-played scene in which the acting out might occur and to review the consequences of acting out. Besides preventing the subsequent pain, it is usually easier to help the client who would act out express his real feelings for the transference object (or the real person) before he has hurt her than it is when he is trying to manage his own pain and repair the damage.

Recognition of Countertransference

A counselor is part of the group and experiences transference too. When the counselor responds to a client as though he is a significant other with whom he has unfinished business, he is experiencing *countertransference*. Usually this occurs when a client looks or behaves like the counselor's transference object and/or is trying to deal with a problem that also is an unresolved problem for the counselor. Obviously, an effective counselor must be able to detect countertransference, disengage, and use the problem it implies to help his client.

Korner (1950) believes that there are several distinct signs that point to a counselor's experiencing transference. When he has difficulty focusing his attention on what a client is saying, is insensitive to a client's needs, cannot seem to comprehend what a client is trying to communicate, is suddenly distracted by thoughts unrelated to a client's words, becomes impatient with a client's progress or a client's willingness to disclose personal information or feelings, feels at a loss concerning how to help a client, or tries to protect a client from pain, he is probably experiencing transference. Cohen's (1952) guidelines for detecting countertransference are similar to Korner's: unreasoning dislike, dread of the treatment period with him, excessive liking for him, undue concern about him between sessions, feeling angrily sympathetic with him, inability to empathize with him, overemotional reactions to his troubles, defensiveness, argumentativeness, indifference, inattentiveness, and impatience.

Whenever a counselor detects such feelings and is unable to disengage himself sufficiently to use his data to formulate helpful responses, he should consider listening to relevant sections of the recording of the group session with a trusted colleague or supervisor in order to determine whether he distorted communication or intensified resistance, to appraise his management of the therapeutic process, to identify any unfinished business on which he should initiate work, and to determine whether he requires professional help to master his personal problem. Countertransference distracts the counselor's attention away from his helping role, distorts his communications with clients, and interferes with his management of resistance (Goodman, Marks, & Rockberger, 1964).

Management of Countertransference

Usually when a counselor realizes that he is experiencing countertransference during a group session, he can merely sit back until he "tunes in" again. Sometimes he may wish to have someone review what was said during the period when he was distracted by countertransference. Occasionally he will feel that sharing the circumstances of the countertransference will facilitate the therapeutic process and help him to disengage from the countertransference.

When Andrew discussed the problems which he and his children experienced when his wife went back to work, the counselor experienced countertransference. However, he discovered these feelings early and recognized why he was beginning to feel angry towards Jane, Andrew's wife. He owned these feelings and spoke as follows to the members of his couples' group:

> This is a problem for me, too, Andrew. My wife has gone back to work recently, and our children and I are having problems with it. Moreover, I believe that sharing this will enable me to focus on helping both Andrew and Jane, but your special assistance would be appreciated. Don't let me take Andrew's side.

In other words, the counselor must detect countertransference, do what is required to disengage himself, and once again participate more therapeutically in the group. Following such a session, he listens to that section of the tape, and often what occurred just before that point, to determine what precipitated countertransference, to decide what he must do to handle it better next time, and to decide whether he should critique that session with a colleague.

Many countertransference situations can be considerably more complex. In one case the situation was complicated by the fact that, in addition to being threatened by a hostile client,

Bob, the counselor had difficulty deciding whether Bob was just a person with a lot of hostility, was responding to him—the counselor—as a negative transference object, or was a negative transference object for himself (the counselor). In this instance Chuck, a group member, developed the courage to interrupt Bob's criticism of Dorothy, who was not Bob's wife, to discuss his disappointment with his son's behavior. The counselor said, "You wish that he'd try harder and let you help him make something out of his life." Bob cut off Chuck's attempted reponse with this response to the counselor: "So you think college is so great too—that college graduates are better than the rest of us." Although the actual response was mild compared to many of his outbursts, the entire group reacted angrily for almost fifteen minutes and told him off. Bob stood up and threatened to walk out and quit. The counselor stood up, paused for several minutes, and responded as follows:

> Bob, I can understand why the others have responded to you as they just did. In fact I am pleased that they are not bullied by you anymore, but I would like you to stay if you are willing to try to talk about the things that really bother you and to learn some essential new behaviors. You upset me, too. When I try to guess how you really feel and help you discuss your real pain, you deny it—like you are afraid to own it and work on it. I think that you really hurt and that you would like to be a better husband and father, but you are afraid to appear weak and vulnerable. Of course, that does take real courage. Perhaps you don't have it or you are afraid you don't have it. In spite of your mean, distracting behavior, I'd like to give you another chance to notice how your fellow clients are able to admit where they hurt, discuss their pain openly, and learn new behaviors rather than watch for a chance to attack and to put others down. I'd like your fellow clients to invite you to stay, too, to give you considerate feedback, to teach you to listen to it and use it—both on what they think you should work on and on what they like from you when they are trying to get help for themselves.

There was another long pause. Bob still stood at the door.
Then the counselor said, "If you are willing to work, sit

down and let the group tell you the conditions under which they are willing to let you stay."

For the first time Bob appeared subdued and willing to listen. Every member of the group, including his aggressive wife, gave him considerate feedback. Then the group asked Bob to discuss what was really worrying him right then and who was upsetting him. With whom did he have unfinished business and with whom would he initiate action to complete this business this week? Of course, he still blew up occasionally, but no longer did he threaten other members to the same degree that he had in the past.

In Bob's case it seemed to be productive for the counselor to share his own real feelings briefly, and to use the sharing to disengage sufficiently to invite Bob to stay—under the appropriate conditions—and to ask the group to decide whether or not Bob should stay. Had the other clients encouraged the counselor to deal more thorougly with his feelings for Bob or to reveal with whom he had unfinished business, he would have indicated briefly how he consults colleagues to detect whether or not he has unfinished business and to decide whether or not he needs therapy—and, of course, to seek therapy if he does need it. Then he would have indicated that this is their therapeutic time and that while he wants them to know when he is hurting and appreciates their special assistance on such occasions, they should use most of the time for dealing with their own problems.

Some counselors tend to overreact to clients who make them feel angry or hostile. Wilson (1974) claims that counselors must be sensitive to the impact that clients can have on them and to understand and accept it in order to manage anger or hostility effectively in a group. Suicidal patients, in particular, tend to arouse countertransference hatred in a counselor (Maltsberger & Buie, 1974). When a counselor denies or distorts countertransference hatred, he increases the danger of a patient's suicide.

The counselor must accept the fact that he is not perfect and will not always experience unconditional positive regard for every client. Although he is committed to continue to grow personally as well as professionally, he will experience countertransference. Therefore, he must learn to detect and manage it. By recording every session he collects the essential data for detecting and analyzing even the incidents that he misses during counseling. Good supervision is essential to detect countertransference, to manage it, to use the new insights uncovered by its study, to help the counselor discover unfulfilled needs, unresolved problems, and unfinished business, and to encourage his personal growth. Whereas clients do get upset when they detect a counselor exhibiting favoritism or letting a client suffer needlessly, they can accept countertransference as a part of his being human, especially when a counselor openly solicits their assistance in detecting it and managing it, as Andrew's counselor did.

Summary

A client is exhibiting transference when he assigns a person the role of a significant other with whom he has unfinished business and reacts to him as if he were that significant other. Rather than explaining why a client does this, it is more important to help a client express his feelings for transference objects in the group and learn to cope with whatever problems evolve before he practices new skills for dealing with target persons outside the group.

With the emphasis placed upon the client's responsibility for identifying his own pain, defining his own goals, and implementing his own desired new behaviors, nothing special is done to elicit transference. It still occurs and should be accepted as a normal outgrowth of the counseling process.

When the counselor experiences transference with clients it is called countertransference. Counselors must learn to detect it, disengage, and become engaged again in the therapeutic process. Sometimes a counselor requires the assistance of a trusted colleague or supervisor to detect countertransference, to manage it, and to achieve his own desired growth.

Questions to Think About

1. What can a counselor learn from the client who is tempted to act out? How can he use acting out to help the client complete his unfinished business? Why should the counselor try to help him cope with material before he acts out? Why should a counselor try to prevent acting out?

2. Think of a time when you experienced transference. Use this to identify the unfinished business you have to complete

with the person who was the object of the transference.
3. Why focus the client's attention on the feelings being transferred rather than on the object with whom he has unfinished business?
4. Explain how management of clients' dependency influences development of transference within a counseling group.
5. Why use a reflection rather than an interpretation to help a client manage his transference?
6. What are the consequences of trying to develop permanent relationships with a transference object?
7. What clues may a counselor use to detect transference and countertransference?
8. How may a counselor differentiate between transference reactions and realistic responses to another group member?
9. How may the methods used to select clients and prepare them for group counseling influence the management of transference, the management of resistance, and the prevention and management of acting out?

References

Bach, G. R. Observations on transference and object relations in the light of group dynamics. *The International Journal of Group Psychotherapy*, 1957, 7, 64–76.

Cohen, M. B. Countertransference and anxiety. *Psychiatry*, 1952, 15, 231–243.

Fried, E. Some aspects of group dynamics and the analysis of transference and defenses. *The International Journal of Group Psychotherapy*, 1965, 15, 44–56.

———. Basic concepts in group psychotherapy. In H. I. Kaplan & B. J. Sadock (Eds.), *Comprehensive Group Psychotherapy*. Baltimore: Williams and Wilkins, 1971.

Glatzer, H. T. Aspects of transference in group psychotherapy. *The International Journal of Group Psychotherapy*, 1965, 15, 167–176.

Goodman, M., Marks, M., & Rockberger, H. Resistance in group psychotherapy enhanced by the countertransference reaction of the therapist. *The International Journal of Group Psychotherapy*, 1964, 14, 332–343.

Johnson, A. M., & Szurek, S. A. The genesis of anti-social acting out in children and adults. *Psychiatric Quarterly*, 1952, *21*, 323–343.

Korner, I. J. Ego involvement and the process of disengagement. *Journal of Consulting Psychology*, 1950, *14*, 206–209.

Lieberman, M. A., Yalom, I. D., & Miles, M. D. *Encounter groups: First facts*. New York: Basic Books, 1973.

Maltsberger, J. T., & Buie, D. H. Countertransference hate in the treatment of suicidal patients. *Archives of General Psychiatry*, 1974, *30*, 625–633.

Wilson, J. Transference and counter-transference in counseling. *British Journal of Guidance and Counseling*, 1974, *2*, 15–26.

Yalom, I. D. *The theory and practice of group psychotherapy*. New York: Basic Books, 1975.

Ziferstein, I., & Grotjahn, M. Group dynamics of acting out in analytic group psychotherapy. *International Journal of Group Psychotherapy*, 1957, *7*, 77–85.

8

RESISTANCE TO CHANGING

Clients who have experienced the type of presentation and intake interviews described earlier in this book exhibit less resistance and assume more responsibility for coping with it than clients who have been less carefully prepared for counseling. Nevertheless, some still fail to cooperate fully in the therapeutic process. These clients try to avoid facing certain kinds of pain and implementing certain new behaviors: they want to cooperate fully in the therapeutic process, yet they resist change. When they feel this way during individual counseling, they may arrive late for an appointment, skip sessions, postpone appointments, appear unable to openly discuss what really worries and upsets them, dwell on their case history, become preoccupied with side issues or small talk, act distracted or confused, act out, demand or plead for advice, avoid or evade the definition of precise behavioral goals and criteria which they can use to appraise their own progress, act spontaneously cured (flight to health), or escape further treatment by dropping out. Besides those behaviors that resisting clients exhibit in individual counseling, there are additional ones that they exhibit in groups: advice giving, protective talking, monopolizing, selective silences, complaining about one's spouse, editing one's spouse's reports, talking about persons outside the group rather than themselves and their own pain, questioning whether the group is a safe place to talk and/or whether others will really keep confidences, and acting overwhelmed by their responsibilities for their own growth, others' growth, or developing and maintaining a therapeutic climate.

Some do not even seem to be conscious of their own resistance. When, therefore, they are confronted by a counselor's interpretation of their resisting behaviors, they tend to deny them. Perhaps that is why a resisting client prefers reflection to interpretation—why the helper's effort to nonjudgmentally guess how he feels facilitates his discussion of those feelings that are the source of his resistance.

The Client's Point of View

Even a client who has contracted to change and has defined goals to achieve change may wonder whether he can achieve his own goals with reasonable effort, or whether they are worth the effort. Sally's situation is a good illustration of this situation. Sally and Jim both seemed to want to salvage their marriage when they joined a couples' group. As they struggled with their problems, especially their sexual dysfunctioning, it became increasingly clear that Sally (a young M.D.) wanted better sex, but not necessarily with Jim (a hospital administrator who was ten years older than she was and looked even older). When they married, Sally had had very few dates with anyone else and did not remember herself as ever being very attractive. She admired Jim and was proud of his success. Then they moved near a major university campus, and she was admitted to medical school.

During medical school Jim was a good source of en-

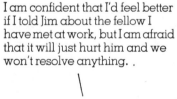

couragement as well as emotional and financial support. But after she received her medical degree, she no longer needed Jim, and other, much younger men were attracted to her. However, the thought of dumping Jim was painful to her and devastating to Jim. Her ambivalence increased even further when one of the other members, an attorney, pointed out to Jim that at least he should be able to make a case for an attractive financial settlement. Furthermore, the other three women rallied to Jim's support with feedback on his strengths, helped him own and discuss openly his pain, and with the counselor's assistance defined precise new behaviors, including expressing and developing the skills required to achieve greater intimacy with a woman. They also encouraged Sally to discuss her own real pain and the new behaviors that she would have to master to achieve a meaningful partnership with him or anyone else. In spite of the women's anger with Sally and the undue amount of time spent on this couple for three sessions, the experience seemed to increase the group's cohesiveness and to encourage the other three couples to communicate on a more genuine level and to deal with conflict more openly.

Even committed clients sometimes ask themselves questions such as:

1. Is this matter really that important?
2. Does this problem really worry or upset me enough to justify the pain that I now experience in discussing it; or am I willing to suffer that much to discuss this problem here?
3. Will the other members really continue to accept me when they discover what I did, said, or what I am really like?
4. Can I handle that much pain when the real problem is uncovered?
5. Is there a possibility that in the course of discussing this problem I may uncover still worse deficiencies in myself and/or my mate?
6. After I have faced the pain will I be able to learn and implement the desired new behaviors?
7. If I really face my pain and make myself vulnerable, is my mate apt to insist that I make still more difficult changes?

These are usually the resisting client's private fears that block his self-disclosure and threaten him when he contemplates learning desired new behaviors. Rather than explain why he feels as he does and elects to avoid the related pain, counselors who use this model prefer to try to detect how the resisting client feels and say it for him. Furthermore, early in the therapeutic relationship the counselor describes the phenomenon of resistance in these terms for clients and explains why it is important for them to help each other recognize it, formulate reflections to facilitate its discussion, help the resisting client to decide where he can begin to cope with the unfinished business associated with this particular resistance, and, when he still is tempted to resist, to examine the consequences of doing nothing now.

The first time the counselor detects an example of a client's resistance, she empathizes with the resisting client to capture precisely the fears that he is experiencing, uses a reflection to facilitate his discussion of his fears, and reinforces his attempts

to overcome them. (This process also provides a model for helping a client deal with his own resistance and teaches clients to do this for each other.) The more accurately the counselor concretely reflects what fears the client is experiencing and enlists fellow clients' encouragement to express them, the more effective she is in helping a client learn to cope with his own resistance. After the first time she has had some success in helping an individual client cope with his own resistance, the counselor may wish to describe resistance to the group, tell why it occurs, explain why she used these helping techniques, how they can detect when it is happening, and why it is important for them to help each other manage their own resistance.

Sometimes a client will recognize his own resistance and conclude that he requires an individual conference to cope with it. On such an occasion, the counselor should encourage the client to make such a request during the group session. Several benefits accrue from such discussions in the group:

1. As the client presents his case for a private conference and explains why he is unable to discuss this particular problem, he often discovers the encouragement and support he needs from the group and discusses what he was avoiding.

2. The discussion clarifies for other clients the purpose for such a conference—to prepare one's self to discuss the problem within the group rather than to use the private conferences to escape from the fear of being rejected.

3. It prevents the "sibling" rivalry that can develop when clients conclude that one of their members is getting preferred treatment. Though occasionally an individual conference may be used to help a client get ready to discuss a problem in the group, the client should look upon the group as his primary source of help.

The techniques described in Chapters 3 and 4 present clients with the information they need to decide for themselves whether to participate in group counseling, to get themselves ready for counseling, and to make essential commitments for their own growth, including coming to the first session prepared to discuss their own real pain openly. Thus, each client is prepared in the intake interview to begin the very first session discussing his own most difficult problems, and he usually has been reinforced for doing so before he has had to cope with resistance. All of these facilitate genuine feeling of

belonging and cohesiveness within the group and encouragement to admit resistance. Perhaps the most powerful
encouragement for an individual to recognize and to manage
his own resistance is other group members' admiration.

Adequate structuring includes the counselor's early recognition of resistance; the precise recognition of what the client is
feeling, reflecting accurately, and helping him manage it; an
explanation to other group members of how he determined
what the client's underlying resisting feelings were (encouraging the client to correct him when he is wrong); and an explanation of why it is important for them to recognize and help other
clients manage resistance. Appropriate structuring and clarification of expectations help clients cope with resistance by
striking a delicate balance, providing just enough structure to
facilitate therapeutic talk without overstructuring. Intense com-
petition develops when there is too little structure and clients
tend to become inhibited by too much structure (Powdermaker
& Frank, 1953).

Group Resistance

Occasionally all or most clients experience resistance simultaneously. Usually this occurs when all or most clients share a
common problem and fear that they can't cope with it. When
the counselor detects the likelihood of such an event occurring
as he is interviewing clients for admission to the group, he
discusses the problem with one or two of the most prestigious
members, explains the danger of group resistance, and helps
them make the commitment to model open discussion of this
particular pain and implementation of desired new behaviors.

Yalom (1975) describes a technique that he uses to cope
with resistance in his groups:

> I never cease to be awed by the rich lode of subter-
> ranean data which exists in every group and in every
> meeting. Beneath each sentiment expressed there are
> layers of invisible, unvoiced ones. How to tap these
> riches? Sometimes when there is a long silence in a
> meeting I express this very thought: "There is so much
> information that could be available to us all today if
> only we could excavate it. I wonder if we could, each

of us, tell the group about some thoughts that occurred to us in this silence which we thought of saying but didn't." The exercise is more effective, incidentally, if the therapist himself starts it or participates. For example, "I've been feeling antsy in the silence, wanting to break it, not wanting to waste time, but on the other hand feeling irritated that it always has to be me doing this work for the group," or "I've been feeling torn between wanting to get back to the struggle between you and me, Mike. I feel uncomfortable with this much tension and anger, but I don't know, yet, how to help understand and resolve it." When I feel there has been a particularly great deal unsaid in a meeting, I have often used, with success, a technique such as this: "It's now six o'clock and we still have half an hour left, but I wonder if you each would imagine that it is already six thirty and that you're on your way home. What kind of disappointments would you have about this meeting today?" (pp. 137–138).

Another variation of Yalom's technique is to ask each client to close his eyes and imagine what private pain each group member would share if the group could make it truly safe for him to do so. The counselor asks everyone to think especially about what the primary clients were discussing just before the uncomfortable silence.

Still another variation is to have the couple whose problems were being discussed when resistance developed use role reversal to unlock the resistance. When, for example, resistance developed while the husband (Darrell) was talking, the counselor prepared the couple as follows:

Anita, close your eyes and imagine yourself in Darrell's role. Visualize yourself actually inside his skin and experiencing his pain. When you are ready, let us know. Then, Darrell, you take Anita's role. As Anita, listen to her very carefully—helping her in *your role* to express the pain that she believes you must express, to identify the persons with whom you have unfinished business, and to define precise behavioral goals you need to complete your unfinished business. Whenever either fails to express adquately what he or she is experiencing in that role, please get up, stand behind the appropriate person and use the alter ego format to express that material for him or her.

When Anita had accomplished what she felt that she could, the group processed the role-played experience (Chapter 6), beginning with Darrell sharing what he discovered about himself and how he felt about it, and inviting the group to give him feedback. In particular he asked the group whether they agreed with Anita's perception of his pain and unfinished business. Then they repeated the role-played scene, with Darrell discussing his problems as he perceived them and Anita being his special helper, and processed that scene. By that time the group was active again, others were ready to work, and, hence, they did not feel any further need to continue discussing Darrell's resistance.

Still another approach involves getting group members to identify the point at which group resistance was first detected and to review that section of the tape. (Since nonverbal behavior is usually very revealing, it is very helpful to have video recordings of such sessions.) The counselor may initiate such a

I wonder what really worries Darrell, and why he can't discuss it with me?

I wonder whether she has guessed that we are in trouble with our creditors.

review of the tape with a comment such as "Let's rewind the tape to a spot a few minutes before the point where we first noticed resistance and try to identify what triggered it and figure out what we should say to whom to facilitate his discussion of his resistance fears. Also look for any behaviors that suggest that someone was avoiding rather than dealing directly with pain."

Frequently, all that is required is for the counselor to recognize in an early session the clues which suggest group resistance, explain why the phenomenon occurs, and explain why it is important for clients to accept responsibility for managing it. A comment such as the following usually helps clear the air:

> When I talked to you in the presentation and your intake interviews, you confided that this is a painful problem for you to discuss, but you seemed to realize that it is something that you must discuss now. Even though I realized the danger of including so many of you with a common problem, I decided that each of you was strong enough to discuss your own idiosyncratic resistance fears, and sensitive enough to recognize the genuine support offered by the group, to face your problems here. I am convinced that you have what it takes to deal with your problems here. Are you sufficiently convinced to proceed or are you going to throw in the towel and give up?

Sometimes in one of the early sessions, clients behave as though they are experiencing group resistance when they merely require clarification of expectations. Therefore, when in doubt about this matter, the counselor may wish to have a volunteer review what is expected of members as both clients and as helpers. On the other hand, the counselor may discover that clients really know what is expected but that at least some of them doubt that they can achieve what they have bargained for. Those who question their ability to profit from counseling or whether the type of counseling offered is appropriate for them must be helped to discuss their reservations and demonstrate their commitment to discuss their problems openly, to review their goals, to implement their desired new behaviors, and to help others do the same rather than to reinforce their resistance with protective behaviors. Sometimes the group decides that some or even all members require another intake interview to increase their readiness to either profit from the group or leave. When a member elects to drop out, he is encouraged to return to the group to say his good-byes, to solicit feedback and to clarify what his unfinished business is, to discuss the consequences of his decision, and to explore other sources for assistance. Usually even clients who choose to leave are impressed with group members' considerate feedback, and the clarification of expectations and essential commitments enhances therapeutic talk and group cohesiveness. Even when the group terminates without members achieving their goals, the occasion can be used productively to help members get in touch with unfinished business and to identify other sources of professional assistance.

Counselor Involvement With Resistance

It is easy to see why a client experiences resistance as a consequence of internal forces, but resistance can also come from external forces. When a counselor experiences countertransference, he may induce resistance, reinforce it, distract a client from relevant therapeutic concerns, and/or distort perceptions of those concerns (Goodman, Marks, & Rockberger, 1964). As a consequence of two and a half years of peer supervision designed to improve their management of resistance, Goodman, Marks, and Rockberger concluded as follows:

> The procedure in these sessions was for one of the therapists to choose for presentation and discussion the group which was not meeting his expectation for movement and in which he was encountering stiff resistance. The presenter would often present a tape recording of a session of his problem group, and his colleagues would question his interventions as well as the meaning of the interaction of group members. They would speak of the feeling they got as they listened to the session, and the presenting therapist would speak of what he saw as the resistance. The focus would then shift to some excess or lack of effective response in the presenter, a particular defensive attitude or position, and the feelings and reactions of

his colleagues. . . . As we studied our countertransference to our groups, our patients, and each
other, we became increasingly aware that these in
turn induced reactions in our patients and led, at
times, to seemingly inpenetrable resistance phenomena within our therapy groups. . . .

We would, therefore, hypothesize that the phenomenon of a therapy group in a state of resistance
which the therapist recognizes but is unable to deal
with is likely to be related integrally to a countertransference distortion of the therapist. The therapist becomes bound up in affects related to his personal past,
which are inappropriate to his current situation, and
he cannot act constructively. We have no doubt that
many premature terminations of treatment are based
on such phenomena.

We have found the peer supervisory group an
excellent setting in which to bring into consciousness
many of the binding images which interfere with our
work. As was noted in the clinical examples, the peer
supervisory group often mirrors the complex forces
operative in the therapeutic group situation, and as
such may be more immediately helpful than the di-
dactic supervisory relationship, which is more para-
digmatic of the individual treatment situation (pp. 335-
336; 343).

Even better results can be obtained when peers use video
instead of audio tapes to help the counselor discover precisely
how his countertransference, lack of congruence, or failure to
recognize and deal more appropriately with a client's resistance (or even group resistance) stymied the group's progress.
Obviously, careful analysis of video tapes with a peer and/or
supervisor can help the counselor detect countertransference
distractions and use these private reactions therapeutically
during counseling. The counselor can also enlist his colleague's assistance in answering questions such as, Why is the
resisting client having this impact on me now? What unfinished
business does it reveal I have with someone? How can I use
these data to respond more effectively to this client?

Most counselors and therapists have had trouble accepting the resisting client. At least occasionally they have reacted personally to the resisting client's antitherapeutic behaviors and felt rejected, unappreciated, frustrated, and angry. On such occasions, it helps for the counselor to remember that, except when the counselor is a negative transference object, the uncooperative response usually is not directed at the counselor. More often than not, the client is caught up in an internal struggle—wanting to change but fearing the consequences of trying to change. When, therefore, he is functioning well, a counselor can review what happened prior to the point of resistance, enlist other clients' assistance in figuring out what the resisting client is experiencing, and reflect the resisting client's underlying fear. In general, the other techniques presented in this chapter also stressed helping clients to recognize and manage their own resistance with the assistance and encouragement of fellow clients rather than having the counselor accept primary responsibility for managing resistance.

Summary

Resistance is the failure to cooperate in the therapeutic process. Clients exhibit resistance when they question whether it is necessary to face the pain involved in discussing their problems, whether they will fall apart during the struggle, whether they can learn the essential new behaviors, or whether the treatment they are getting will be effective. It may be precipitated by the counselor's inept or hurtful behavior and countertransference. Though at times it may seem to be directed against the counselor this usually is not the intent. Usually it results from the resisting client's internal conflict of wanting what he bargains for but doubting whether he can achieve it.

When clients are properly selected and prepared for group counseling, they usually have discussed their real concerns and have been reinforced for doing so before they experience difficult resistance. Usually it is profitable for the counselor to briefly describe the phenomenon of resistance, explain why it occurs, how one can recognize it within himself and in others, and how it can be used to help the resisting client to uncover new unfinished business. By the time resistance usually occurs, clients also have had some successful experiences detecting how another feels and helping him say it; therefore, they can see readily how to use the same methods to facilitate discussion of the resisting client's fears of change—especially after they have seen their counselor do it and heard him explain what he is doing, why he uses the technique, and how he uses it to help. Thus, the counselor displays teaching and partnership roles—helping group members to understand the phenomenon and to help the resisting client to discuss his fears, to discover that he can endure them, and to decide with what mini-goals he can begin to implement desired new behaviors.

Questions to Think About

1. How may the method of selecting couples contribute to resistance in a group? How may it facilitate the management of resistance?
2. What specifically could you as a counselor do to minimize the instances of resistance in a marriage counseling group?
3. What criteria would you use to detect resistance in a marriage counseling group?
4. Why do so many counselors seem to perceive the resisting client's reactions as a personal reflection on them? How could you use these reactions to determine where to begin the management of resistance in a particular group or to detect new therapeutic material?
5. How can structuring be used to prevent resistance in a group?
6. Think of a specific instance in which you sought assistance with a problem and then resisted the help that was offered. How did fear inhibit your open discussion of the problem and/or implementation of desired new behaviors? Formulate a reflection that a counselor could have used to help you manage your own resistance.
7. Explain how acting out interferes with a client's successful management of his resistance.
8. How may a counselor help group members establish and maintain therapeutic group norms? How do such group norms facilitate clients' recognition and management of resistance?

9. For what purposes would you encourage a client to schedule an intensive intake-type interview during counseling? Explain how you would introduce the idea and prepare the resisting client for the interview.
10. What criteria could you use to differentiate between the resistance caused by counselor's countertransference, client transference, and client's ambivalence concerning outcomes of discussing his problem openly?
11. How may a counselor use resistance therapeutically in a counseling group?

References

Goodman, M., Marks, M., & Rockberger, H. Resistance in group psychotherapy enhanced by countertransference reactions of therapist: A peer group experience. *International Journal of Group Psychotherapy*, 1964, *14*, 332–343.

Powdermaker, F. B., & Frank, J. D. *Group psychotherapy*. Cambridge: Harvard University Press, 1953.

Yalom, I. D. *The theory and practice of group psychotherapy*. New York: Basic Books, 1975.

9

DEVELOPING AND MAINTAINING INTIMACY

Everyone needs close, intimate relationships with a partner for whom he cares deeply, with whom he enjoys exciting, satisfying sex, with whom he experiences genuine rich companionship, with whom he can share his successes and pleasures and discuss his failures and disappointments, and from whom he can seek assistance when confronted with problems. Most persons who seek marriage counseling hope to develop such a relationship with their spouse.

Some clients wonder whether intimacy can be achieved in our rapidly changing, mobile society. Perhaps they have concluded that the increased divorce rate is a flight from intimacy. Bach and Deutch (1970) reject this idea. On the contrary, they believe that most couples split because partners failed to find the intimacy desired. Bach and Wyden (1970) believe that people try marriage again and again to achieve the intimacy they require.

When persons fail to achieve a modicum of satisfying, meaningful intimacy, they tend to become discouraged and depressed. They suffer from loneliness, lack of support during crises, unsatisfied "skin hunger," and loss of hope for the future. Couples who do not achieve for themselves a minimum degree of intimacy tend to replace the striving for intimacy with anger and disappointment, and sexual dysfunctioning often occurs.

Family Influence

Families are people makers. Satir (1972) describes the atmosphere in troubled families: "self-worth [is] low; communication [is] . . . vague and not really honest; rules [are] rigid, inhuman, nonnegotiable, and everlasting; and linking to society [is] fearful, placating, and blaming" (pp. 3–4). She contrasts this with the very different atmosphere in nurturing families: "self-worth is high; communication is direct, clear, specific, and honest; rules are flexible, human, appropriate and subject to change; and the linking to society is open and hopeful" (p. 4).

The role played by the family obviously makes the important difference in the development of the individual. Nurturing families help each member develop into

a physically healthy, mentally alert, feeling, loving, playful, creative human being; one who can stand on his own two feet, who can love deeply and fight fairly and effectively, who can be on equally good terms with both tenderness and toughness, knows the difference between them, and therefore struggles effectively to achieve his goals. . . .

Immediately, I can sense the aliveness, the genuineness, honesty, and love. I feel the heart and soul present as well as the head.

I feel that if I lived in such a family, I would be listened to and would be interested in listening to others; I would be considered and would wish to consider others; I could openly show my affection as well as my pain and disapproval; I wouldn't be afraid to take risks because everyone in my family would realize that some mistakes are bound to come with my risk taking—that my mistakes are a sign that I am growing. I would feel like a person in my own right—noticed, valued, loved, and clearly asked to notice, value, and love others.

The house where these people live tends to have a lot of light and color. It is clearly a place where people *live*, planned for their comforts and enjoyment, not a show-place for the neighbors.

People seem comfortable about touching one another and showing their affection, regardless of age. The evidence of loving and caring isn't limited to carrying out the garbage, cooking the meals, or bringing home the paycheck. People show it also by talking openly and listening with concern, by being straight and real with one another, by simply being together.

Members of a nurturing family feel free to tell each other how they feel. Anything can be talked about—

the disappointments, fears, hurts, angers, criticisms as well as joys and achievements (Satir, 1972, pp. 3, 13–14).

In other words, persons who grow up in these families, or join them later as adults and adapt to them, learn to be intimate, to appreciate and accept intimacy, and to enhance intimate relationships within their families.

Until the last couple of generations most whose fear of intimacy was greater than their need for it tended not to marry. Fifty years ago almost one-fifth of all people never married. Now all but 6.5 percent of women and 7 percent of men have married at least once (Bach and Wyden, 1970). Bach and Wyden described persons who tend to fail in marriage as follows:

> Mostly they are misguided idealists who yearn for sweet but empty harmony instead of honest relationship where the normal hostilities of each partner are aired so there will be more love and understanding, rather than less, as the years go by. . . . Pseudointimates wear masks and play games. Their marriages become predictable and boring. . . .
>
> True familiarity, on the other hand, is forever fascinating because the human brain can, and does, meet any situation in an endless variety of ways. Children tend to display this wonderful creative responsiveness before parents teach them to be on guard against openness and transparency. No wonder we must teach adults to learn to let their guard down, at least when they are dealing with loved ones (p. 35).

In addition to helping couples achieve intimacy for themselves, marriage counseling in groups should prepare participating adults to model intimate, nurturing behaviors such as Satir describes and help their own families create an atmosphere in which intimacy is experienced, accepted, and learned. Parent education (Clark-Stewart, 1978; Dreikurs & Soltz, 1974; Gordon, 1970; Patterson, 1976) and marriage enrichment programs (Calvo, 1973; Hopkins & Hopkins, 1976; Mace & Mace, 1977; Overturf, 1976; Regula, 1975; Travis & Travis, 1975) also have helped reasonably healthy couples enhance the development of such nurturing families. On the other hand, some families require extensive family counseling over a long period of time in order to develop into nurturing families (Dreikurs, Gould, & Corsini, 1974; Haley, 1976; Minuchin, 1974; Satir, 1967, 1972).

Since intimacy is learned, even troubled families can be helped to learn it. While it is difficult for those who did not experience it as children to learn it as adults, it is not impossible. Even in reasonably healthy couples' groups, some people question whether or not it is worth the pain and effort to admit their need for intimacy and to learn to enjoy it until other group members are able to help them explore the consequences for themselves and their children of giving up and doing nothing. And, as Bach and Wyden (1970) point out, intimacy is a skill that must be learned:

> People think that it is incongruous that intimacy needs to be taught. We point out to them that it is not a birthright or a talent, like a musical ear. It is probably the most civilized relationship within the capability of mankind. Furthermore, it is a conscious choice. Man must want to be intimate; the choice is up to him and intimacy can be achieved only when intimates rub the rough edges of their personalities against one another (p. 35).

Negotiating Intimacy

Those who seek marriage counseling are striving for intimacy and at the same time fearing it or, at least, not knowing how to accept it, enjoy it, and manage it. They want all the advantages that accrue from a close, intimate, trusting marriage partnership, but many also fear being used, swallowed up, and controlled. From time to time they also may discover that true intimacy can be exhausting (Bach and Wyden, 1970). Healthy, adequate persons want a loving and sexually satisfying partnership in which they experience "oneness" and at the same time are permitted, and encouraged, to develop into separate, self-sufficient, lovable human beings.

Marriage partners have had their own individual pasts, and they grew up in at least somewhat different homes in which degree of intimacy and the way it is expressed varied. Thus, each must learn to discuss his need for intimacy with his mate, to request it, to accept it, and to be sensitive to his spouse's need for it and fear of it. Figure 1 can be used to show couples how to begin this negotiation process. The spaces indicate the following: A is restricted for only the most trusted intimates; B is reserved for close friends; C is for friends; D is for acquaintances; and E is for strangers and unknowns. Enemies very likely can be placed anywhere between A and D. They have hurt us and perhaps are in a position to hurt us again (e.g., a former spouse and parent to our children, former employer or employee, etc.). They also may be persons whom we have hurt or neglected.

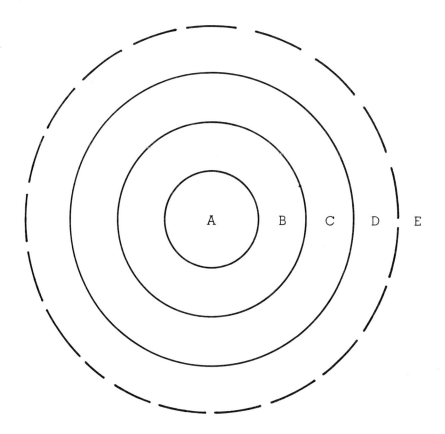

Figure 1. Intimacy Levels

Some people reserve A for themselves and an occasional invited guest—even a spouse does not know when he can expect to be included in that space. Others recognize their need for privacy but usually share this intimate space with their spouses, close friends, and relatives. Still others require a larger space for A because they include many intimates. When both spouses place their primary A, B, and C persons on the figure, they can recognize the other's need for intimacy, discuss and negotiate the extent of their need for intimacy, and resolve those conflicts which result from satisfying their differing intimacy needs.

Bach and Wyden (1970) use a technique similar to the approach-avoidance technique described in Chapter 6 for this purpose:

> One amusing but useful at-home exercise begins with the partners conversing while they face each other about 15 feet apart. As they continue to talk, Partner A walks up to Partner B until they make physical contact. Then Partner A slowly backs away until he reaches the right distance to make conversation comfortable for A. At that point A stops and the partners measure the distance between each other with a tape measure. The experiment is repeated with Partner B doing the walking, and backing up. Almost invariably, the partners' distance preferences differ. These measurements, although inexact, suggest each partner's tolerance for closeness. The partner who requires more distance in order to be comfortable is the one who will be more likely to start fights for optimal distance.
>
> "Don't come too close to me" is the message he is signaling (p. 37).

Bach and Wyden reported that many couples disclosed that the morning after particularly satisfying love making, a fight developed over "nothing." Even though the threatened one enjoyed the intimacy, he picked a fight to distance himself.

Following the use of the Bach-Wyden exercise, each participant is encouraged to discuss his feelings concerning his general tolerance for closeness, where he can accept it and enjoy it, and where he finds it most threatening. Taking the spouse's role and replaying the scene also helps each to get in touch with the other's pain and needs, clarifies each other's need for intimacy, and sets the stage for helpful feedback from other group members. Finally, each spouse is encouraged to define desired new behaviors for accepting and enjoying intimacy and for managing it. Frequently role playing is needed to help couples practice and implement these desired new behaviors.

In addition to being afraid of being owned, used, swallowed up, controlled, or abused, some clients fear that intimacy will expose their innate coldness, their inability to love and enjoy intimacy, to cope with touching and love making, or their general inadequacy. The following variation of the approach-avoidance technique can help.

Selected partners are asked to stand and face each other, 15-20 feet apart, then to walk toward each other slowly, discussing the intimate feelings that each has for the other, the additional intimacy that each desires, their fears in seeking it, and their problems of touching each other as they meet. They also are encouraged to use soliloquy (Chapter 6) to communicate the inner, private feelings and thoughts that they are experiencing but are reluctant to express. When it appears that either spouse is harboring feelings that cannot be expressed, even with the use of soliloquy, another client, who has been taught by the counselor, may function as an alter ego and considerately express the feeling that he feels the partner is reluctant to express. Following the processing of the exercise, as is done in other kinds of role playing, the couple is helped to describe the degree of intimacy that each can enjoy now, to negotiate what each would like to learn to do next, and to determine what reinforcement each requires of his spouse to enhance learning of the desired new behaviors.

Another technique, Magic Shop (see Chapter 6), is used to help clients communicate specific intimacy needs and to facilitate discussion of new goals. Usually the counselor asks a spouse to assume his partner's role and bargain with her as the proprietor of the Magic Shop, not for merchandise but for desired new intimacy. After processing the role playing in role reversal, with each spouse in a bargaining role, each spouse is encouraged to reenact the scenes for himself—each functioning as bargainer and shopkeeper. In addition to the usual steps in the final processing, each is asked to answer four questions, and the other clients are encouraged to supplement his answers. What did you discover about your partner's need for intimacy? What did you discover about your own intimacy needs? How can you help her cope with her threats and/or fears and reinforce her successes? With what do the two of you now require assistance in negotiating intimacy needs?

Most couples begin their marriage with hopes and dreams, but many discover early that they are not achieving them and experience disappointment and fear of failure which they often express as anger. Bach and Wyden believe that the way to help them is to teach them to fight fairly. Mace (1976) rejects Bach and Wyden's approach and tries instead to help couples recognize the early signs of anger and to manage it. Furthermore, he believes that encouraging fighting intensifies the anger:

> Thinking over what has happened in all these marriages, I have asked myself some basic questions. What is it, above all else, that prevents so many marriages from achieving the warm, loving, mutually creative experiences the partners hope and long for? Some say it is sexual maladjustment. Others say temperamental incompatibility, or poor role functioning, or inadequate communication, or adverse environmental pressures. There are many theories. I have

I wish I knew how to ask for them.

considered them all—and rejected them all in favor of something that is hardly ever mentioned. My conclusion is that what causes marriages to fail, over and over again, is the incapacity of the couple to cope with their own and each other's anger. . . .

What they want is love. In order to get it, they seek intimacy. As they move closer to each other, something happens. Differences between them, which seemed unimportant or even attractive when viewed from a distance, now become threatening and cause disagreement. This happens inevitably when people enter into a shared life. They are now in a dilemma. Should they move away from each other to ease the disagreement? No, because they want intimacy, and that means moving closer. So they move closer. Then the disagreement becomes more painful. It heats up and becomes conflict—the loving couple find a flood of negative feelings being stirred up—hostility, irritation, disillusionment. All of which create anger. These negative feelings destroy the warm loving feelings with which they approached each other. They feel cheated (pp. 131, 132).

Both Mace and Bach and Wyden are right. Couples must be taught to recognize early the pain which is expressed as anger and to cope with the anger; they also must learn to fight fairly. Perhaps most important of all, each must learn to request the intimacy he needs, to accept it, to enjoy it, and to negotiate for the degree of intimacy with which each can cope at the present. Couples also must learn to cope with a variety of critical junctures (passages) and/or developmental tasks and experience at various stages in their marriage.

Managing passages

After one couple has dealt successfully with a passage and reviewed what they have learned from that particular experience, the counselor may use their experience to introduce the general problem of passages. Just listing some passages on the blackboard clarifies the notion and encourages couples to share problems more spontaneously with each other.

Listed next are passages commonly reported by marriage counseling clients.

- Developing a genuine partnership
- Recognizing and managing power struggles
- Managing the first serious conflict
- Achieving independence and maintaining intimacy with one's family and in-laws
- Changing careers, reviewing career plans, and/or coping with unemployment and/or underemployment
- Deciding how to cope with a promotion for one partner that influences negatively the other's career
- Accidental pregnancies
- Deciding on whether to have children
- Adjusting to children and learning to manage them
- Adjusting to family crises such as serious illness, death, and disappointments with children
- Changing communities
- Terminating responsibilities for children and learning to live together alone after the children leave
- Adjusting to retirement and aging

In order to really help a couple, the counselor should encourage the group to help them manage specific passages. Nevertheless, this is not sufficient. They also must help the target couple generalize what they learned from management of one passage and apply it to other situations. Failure to recognize and deal adequately with passages tends to interfere with the development of intimacy and to damage healthy, intimate relationships that seem to be well established.

Successful discussions of passages increases cohesiveness in a marriage counseling group, heightens feelings of affiliation among clients, encourages clients to talk more openly, and enhances clients' hope for success. When good self-help materials are available on the passages these can be assigned for cooperative study between counseling sessions.

Communicating the need for intimacy

Because exact language, as well as appropriate nonverbal behavior, is required to communicate intimate messages, intimate communication is difficult. But it can be learned. In order for communication to occur, the sender must be congruent, know what he wants to communicate, know how to convey his message (both with meaningful language and with congruent nonverbal behavior), and have a congruent receiver. Once clients are taught the significance of congruence in communication and how to detect incongruence (see Chapter 5), other clients become very adept at detecting incongruence, helping the speaker talk directly to the target person, using first-person-pronoun messages, and exhibiting appropriate nonverbal behavior that facilitates communication of the *intended* message.

Sometimes couples must be separated, as Mace and Mace (1977) were during World War II, to recognize the full importance of communication. However, they were determined to facilitate enrichment of their relationship in spite of their separation:

> The written word can be cold and lifeless. But it can come alive and glow. It can reach across space that divides one person from another, and communicate warmth and understanding and caring. Letters can do the same. During World War II, we were totally separated for over three years. Those were dangerous years too, and we had no assurance that we would ever see each other, face to face, again. But we could write letters to each other, and we did. We poured out our hearts in some of those letters. Through the written word, we kept our relationship alive, and communicated to each other our faith, our trust, and our imperishable hope. We think our relationship actually grew during those long, grim years of total separation (p. 18).

Some people who live together use written communication to ensure that they communicate precisely what they want to say. Others write their feelings and requests to ensure that they communicate their complete message without interruptions and distractions before they begin their discussion with spouses. For example, Jimmy was a very affectionate husband who was afraid that his ambitious wife (Mavis) would reject him if he ever really let her close to him and shared his real feelings, successes, and failures with her. Even though they usually enjoyed intercourse, he even doubted his ability to satisfy her sexually, and he was very much afraid to share that with her, too. Furthermore, he doubted that she enjoyed sex with him as much as he enjoyed it with her.

Unknowingly Mavis confirmed his worst fears by discuss-

ing how angry she felt when he tried to seduce her with imma-
ture, sweet talk. Following that comment, the counselor said to
Jimmy, "Pretend Mavis is not here, and we will help you write
her a letter in which you incorporate your answers to these
questions: What was the impact of Mavis' comment on you?
How do you really feel toward her? What do you wish that you
could communicate to her convincingly? What peak experiences have you had with her recently? What do you especially
like about her? With which of your goals would you appreciate
her help? How could she more effectively reinforce your mastery of desired new behaviors?"

Then the counselor turned to Mavis and said, "Mavis,
perhaps it would help Jimmy if you would pull your chair out of
the circle where you would be out of Jimmy's line of vision while
he discusses what he wants to include in his letter to you.
Following this discussion the rest of us, including you, Mavis,
will provide Jimmy with feedback."

Then he returned his attention to Jimmy: "Jimmy, would
you feel comfortable working on that letter now?"

Jimmy said it sounded scary, but he would do it. Mavis was
obviously shocked when she heard Jimmy discuss what he
wanted to include in his letter, sensed his tremendous support
in the group, and heard the other clients' convictions concerning Jimmy's sincerity. When Jimmy seemed to be ready to
complete his letter on his own, the counselor checked this out
and got an affirmative answer. Then he asked for reactions to
the experience of helping Jimmy write the letter. The first to
speak was Mavis. She said she was impressed with Jimmy's
sincerity and pointed out that she got the message; Jimmy didn't
have to write the letter. Though Mavis' comments brought forth
a positive response from the other clients, they urged Jimmy to
write the letter, to set aside a specific time to discuss it after
Mavis had a chance to read it and think about it, and to report
their success at the next session. Following their report at the
next session, they were asked to role play specific instances in
which each stood, faced the other, and took a turn in asking for
and responding to requests for intimacy.

After one or two such experiences in which couples have
practiced communication of their needs for intimacy, the counselor can ask each member to inventory his own special needs
for intimacy, order their priority, and decide on which he would

like to initiate specific new behaviors between this session and the next. Over 50 percent of married couples have sexual dysfunctioning problems (see Chapter 2). Thus, requests for sexual intimacy are common, yet sexual intimacy is by no means the only need that is expressed. An inventory of intimacy needs usually will reveal strong needs for identifying other satisfying recreational activities, for time alone together, for time to discuss a variety of topics, and for time to gratify genuine "skin hunger"—to hug and hold one another.

Role playing is often used to help clients ask for and respond to requests for intimacy. It, along with these variations of the approach-avoidance exercises and Magic Shop, can be used effectively to help clients identify and clarify intimacy needs and to practice requesting them. Perhaps more importantly, clients learn to detect and more powerfully express the good feelings they have for each other (e.g., in Jimmy's case above) and to enjoy these good feelings more fully while they are occurring.

Sexual Intimacy

Sex can be an exciting, intimate experience, but it also can be enjoyed for its own sake (Bach & Deutsch, 1970):

> Although it is plain that intimacy-based sex has a far deeper and more significant meaning in the lives of pairers, scientific investigators have had to reject the old idea that sex without intimacy cannot be satisfying or have validity of its own. . . .
>
> In spite of traditional moral disapproval, sex for its own sake, nonintimate sex, is rapidly becoming more common, especially as an exploration by young adults. Temporarily, it can deeply absorb and involve the partners. And from a psychological point of view, it is not damaging provided that it is authentic in its own terms; that is, if neither partner is manipulating or tricking the other into the experience by misrepresenting his feelings. Once again, reality, recognized by oneself and expressed to the other, is the best protection against guilt, anxiety, and anger (p. 220).

Thus, sex cannot be enjoyed fully, even just physically, unless both partners consent and respond openly and honestly to each other as equals. This cannot be achieved when either is seduced or perceived as an object of conquest. It should be used neither to reinforce desired new behaviors nor to reward the other; nor should it be withheld as punishment. Used thus, it tends to damage even well-established, intimate relationships.

The response to intercourse, especially with a new partner, can be unpredictable. Two cases illustrate this point. Bach and Deutsch presented the case of Beverly and Ed, who were developing a good relationship when they went on a weekend house party where they unexpectedly were pressured to share a bedroom with a double bed. Though they had not reached an understanding on sex and neither felt comfortable, they had intercourse and physically enjoyed it; but neither felt good about it. Also, they did not seem to be able to discuss either their reservations about having intercourse or their real feelings about it afterwards. Thus, their growing relationship was seriously damaged. On the other hand, a good sexual experience enhanced Ralph and Betty's relationship. They met at their fortieth high school class reunion. Though they had not dated, they had been good high school friends. Furthermore, they had a great time at the reunion dance. Both had been widowed several years. Ralph asked Betty to have dinner with him the next evening. About lunch time he had a call at his motel from Betty in which she verified their date for 6:30 P.M. and invited him to come by her home that afternoon for a drink—anytime convenient for him. His response was "Great. I'd like to spend a lot of time with you this afternoon. How about 3:30?"

When Ralph arrived, he sensed that he'd communicated well with Betty. She was dressed in an attractive, revealing slack suit and had his drink ready for him. While they sipped their drinks, they discussed their pleasure in meeting each other again, their genuine need for companionship and affection, and their current desire for sex. After Betty owned her feelings, Ralph asked her permission to undress her and to prepare for intercourse in a manner appropriate for the occasion. She agreed. Both enjoyed the intercourse. Neither pretended to be in love. Both knew what they were doing and enjoyed it as such. Everything was open and above board.

They were mutually stimulated, and there was mutual consent. Neither felt pressured to perform or to impress the other. Each felt good about sex and doing it with the other. Thus, their honesty and genuineness enhanced the development of an intimate relationship for them.

A counselor must consider certain basic principles when helping couples with sexual dysfunctioning problems.

1. When he has any suspicions of a client's sexual dysfunctioning problems during the intake interview, he reflects the underlying problem and enlists her spouse's assistance in helping her discuss the pain, fears, and/or threats associated with intercourse. Usually he uses reflections to relate her specific problems to desired new behaviors (goals, including learning to feel comfortable in sharing tender, positive, sexual feelings as well as distracting negative and threatening feelings); helps her spouse capture the depth of her concern and facilitate its discussion with considerate reflections rather than by probing, confronting, or criticizing; and helps her explain what her spouse can do to reinforce her desired new behaviors (see Chapters 1 and 5). Thus, she learns from the beginning of marriage counseling that she can discuss her problems associated with sexual dysfunctioning. When she questions her ability to do so, she is helped to practice discussing it. Furthermore, the counselor tries to locate and include in her group another client who has a similar sexual problem and is committed to discuss it at the beginning of their first group session. Thus, the reluctant client discovers that at least one other person has a similar problem, is helped with it, and doesn't lose face in the group. In fact, she usually discovers that those who can discuss their real problems are reinforced for their courage and provided genuine support. When the counselor isn't certain that the client detects this quality of support, he encourages fellow clients to give her feedback for exhibiting such courage.

2. Where there is a possibility of physical problems that may require medical care, the client is referred for medical examination and, when needed, for essential medical treatment.

3. In general, the counselor should try to help each spouse get ready in the intake interview to discuss sexual dysfunctioning problems, to decide precisely what new feelings and/or behaviors must be established, and to enlist the spouse's assistance in establishing them. Each is helped to accept responsi-

bility for developing the courage to discuss the feelings associated with her sexual dysfunctioning and for coping with them for herself. Furthermore, after she has discussed her most threatening deficiencies and discovered the support she has from both male and female clients in the group, she is encouraged to apply necessary remedial measures and to negotiate the degree of intimacy with which she can cope at present.

When either partner requires special assistance and/or instruction, both are encouraged to read good source materials (Kaplan, 1975; Mace, 1972; Masters & Johnson, 1971; Masters & Johnson, 1976), help each other practice what seem to be the appropriate exercises, and come back to the group to discuss what seemed to work, where they seemed to require assistance, and whether they needed to be scheduled for special sessions with their counselor or to be referred to a sex therapist. Some orgasmic dysfunctioning women can help themselves merely by exploring and stimulating themselves, but others also require nondemand stimulation by a mate (Masters & Johnson, 1971). Some such women tend to be treated most successfully in women's counseling groups with other women (Barbach and Ayres, 1976). Dysfunctioning men tend to require such help as often as women, but are more reluctant to request it. In any case, most dysfunctioning men and women can be helped in counseling groups. Moreover, they tend to profit most from the counseling when they are prepared to take maximum responsibility for getting themselves ready to discuss their pain and to decide what they must do to accept their own sex drive, to enjoy sex, to communicate their need for sexual gratification, and to respond genuinely both verbally and nonverbally during intercourse.

4. Role playing can be used effectively to help clients learn to share sexual feelings, to request intimacy, and to discuss their sexual successes and failures. Role playing also can be used to correct joking put downs and to alleviate the consequent hurts. For example, Norman, a twenty-seven-year-old man who had been married five years, expressed as a joke something that threatened him badly: he lacked source material and confidants to check whether he was becoming impotent. When he was awakened by bladder pressure following a Saturday night beer party and went to the toilet, Candy was awake as he returned to bed. They hugged for several minutes, and both fell asleep. The next morning he realized that was the

first time that he had failed to have intercourse under those circumstances, and though he kidded Candy about it, he was threatened by it. A few days later he lost his erection during foreplay. Then he really became worried, but didn't tell anybody—even other group members. However, when several books were recommended to help couples with their sex problems, he reported how pleased he was to learn that he wasn't the first to experience either of those problems and that it didn't mean that he was becoming impotent. The counselor also used the occasion to have Norman and Candy pull their chairs into the center of the group, to look at each other, and to touch each other while Norman told Candy what he wished he would have shared with her immediately following the second event and what he needed to share with her in the present. Candy was asked to listen to him very carefully and to respond to him in the most helpful way she knew. Both the role playing and the analysis of it substantially helped two other couples as well as Norman and Candy. In fact, it encouraged one couple to role play a similar event in their lives.

5. In order for sex to be most satisfying, there must be mutual consent and genuine respect—real verbal as well as nonverbal sharing. It must not be cheapened by being used as a reward or reinforcer and withheld for punishment.

6. Unfortunately, many partners are hunters. They know how to attract a partner, but they have never learned to maintain and enrich a relationship. When both marriage partners lack partnership development and maintenance skills, they get bored with each other and are tempted to seek excitement, including more exciting sex, with others. In order to develop and maintain a deep, meaningful, intimate partnership each partner must be committed to a growing, developing relationship; recognize early symptoms of conflicts, be committed to solving them, and have the skills and confidence to resolve their conflicts; feel reasonably secure with each other; and enjoy quality companionship as well as sex.

Summary

Intimacy is essential for a healthy human existence. Some have grown up in families whose members accept the need for intimacy, foster its development, and enjoy intimate relationships. Others have grown up in families whose members are distant and cold, recognizing the need for intimacy but also fearing it. People from both kinds of families can learn to express their needs for intimacy, enjoy it, and enhance its development with loved ones.

Even the flight from intimacy suggested by increased divorce rates should not be considered evidence that the human need for intimacy is passé. It is the very opposite. Increasing numbers of persons recognize that even though they may have failed, they believe that they can find a partner with whom they can learn to develop a genuine, intimate, sexually satisfying relationship. Because couples come into marriage from such different backgrounds, they must learn to negotiate the degree of intimacy that each can enjoy and tolerate in the present, to resolve their differences, and to enlist each other's help in implementing those behaviors that will help them become more intimate.

Learning to communicate intimacy needs accurately and genuinely is essential in order to develop and to maintain a meaningful, satisfying relationship. Each partner must learn to use precise language that does not appear to make demands and to respond to requests with sincerity and consideration.

When an individual fails to achieve reasonably satisfying intimacy, he tends to become discouraged and depressed, or to become angry, or to experience sexual dysfunctioning. Often all three occur.

Couples should be prepared and encouraged to discuss their sexual dysfunctioning problems in their counseling group and to accept responsibility for achieving an intimate, satisfying sexual relationship with each other. Discussing these problems openly with other couples, discovering genuine acceptance for dealing with problems directly, deciding precisely what each partner must do, and helping each other implement desired new behaviors genuinely encourages their personal growth. They learn that intercourse can be an exciting, emotional experience for equals and that under satisfactory conditions successful intercourse can enhance intimacy.

Questions to Think About

1. How does one's family influence her chances for the development of a close, intimate relationship with her spouse?
2. What can you as a mature adult do to prepare your children

for a meaningful, intimate, continuing relationship with a marriage partner? What can you do to enlist your spouse's assistance in this process?

3. If you (or one of your children) were courting a prospective mate, what criteria could you use to determine whether that person could help you (or your child) develop a rich, satisfying marriage partnership?

4. Why must a couple negotiate the degree of intimacy that each can enjoy and tolerate?

5. How does Mace's notion of early recognition and management of anger really differ from Bach and Wyden's notion of teaching couples to fight fairly? Is that difference real or illusory?

6. With what passages have you been confronted that damaged your relationship with your spouse? From what you learned in this chapter, what do you wish that you had done differently? With what unfinished business are you still left? What must you do to complete it?

7. What is peculiar about sexual dysfunctioning problems that differentiates them from other intimacy problems with which couples are confronted? What are the key points for a counselor to keep in mind in helping a couple with sex problems?

References

Bach, G. R., & Deutsch, R. M. *Pairing: How to achieve genuine intimacy.* New York: Avon, 1970.

Bach, G. R., & Wyden, P. *The intimate enemy: How to fight fair in love and marriage.* New York: Avon, 1970.

Barbach, L. G., & Ayres, T. Group process for women with orgasmic difficulties. *Personnel and Guidance Journal,* 1976, *54,* 389–391.

Calvo, G. *Marriage encounter.* St. Paul: National Marriage Encounter, 1973.

Clark-Stewart, K. A. Popular primers for parents. *American Psychologists,* 1978, *33,* 359–369.

Dreikurs, R., Gould, S., & Corsini, R. *Family counsel: The Dreikurs technique for putting an end to the war between parents and children.* Chicago: Henry Regnery, 1974.

Dreikurs, R., & Soltz, V. *Children: A challenge.* New York: Hawthorne Books, 1974.

Gordon, T. *Parent effectiveness training.* New York: Peter Wyden Press, 1970.

Haley, J. *Problem solving therapy.* San Francisco: Jossey-Bass, 1976.

Hopkins, P. E., & Hopkins, L. Marriage enrichment and the churches. *Your Church,* 1976, 22, 49-52.

Kaplan, H. S. *The illustrated manual of sex therapy.* New York: Quadrangle, The New York Times Book Co., 1975.

Mace, D. R. *Sexual difficulties in marriage.* Philadelphia: Fortress Press, 1972.

———. Marital intimacy and the deadly love anger cycle. *Journal of Marriage and Family Counseling,* 1976, 2, 131-137.

———. Marriage enrichment: The new frontier. *Personnel and Guidance Journal,* 1977, 55, 520-522.

Mace, D. R., & Mace, V. *How to have a happy marriage.* Nashville: Abingdon Press, 1977.

Masters, W. H., & Johnson, V. E. *Human sexual inadequacy.* Boston: Little, Brown, 1971.

———. *The pleasure bond: A new look at sexuality and commitment.* Boston: Little, Brown, 1976.

Minuchin, S. *Families and family therapy.* Cambridge: Harvard University Press, 1974.

Overturf, J. Marital therapy: Tolerance of differences. *Journal of Marriage and Family Counseling,* 1976, 2, 235-241.

Patterson, G. R. *Living with children: New methods for parents and teachers.* Champaign, Ill.: Research Press, 1976.

Regula, R. R. Marriage encounter: What makes it work? *The Family Coordinator,* 1975, 24, 153-159.

Satir, V. *Conjoint family therapy: A guide to theory and technique.* Palo Alto: Science and Behavior Books, 1967.

———. *Peoplemaking.* Palo Alto: Science and Behavior Books, 1972.

Travis, R. P., & Travis, P. Y. The pairing enrichment program: Actualizing marriage. *The Family Coordinator,* 1975, 24, 161-165.

10

LEARNING COOPERATIVE DECISION MAKING

Today, it is essential for couples, if they are to be happily married, to make decisions cooperatively—as equals. The slave-master relationship no longer works—it probably never really did. Those men who accepted this chauvinistic attitude and made it part of their life outlook were forced to accept complete financial responsibility for their families, tended to be blamed for bad decisions concerning family welfare, experienced undue disappointment and anger when members of the family behaved inappropriately, resented continuing dependency of members, and in general experienced stress. A woman who was married to a chauvinist but was an intelligent and confident individual often used manipulation, conniving, and deceit to influence crucial family decisions. When this attitude was thrust onto a loving, sharing husband who respected his wife's intelligence and judgment, he experienced discomfort and shame. Fortunately, many of these strong husbands who were labeled publicly as masters genuinely respected their wives' judgment and encouraged their participation privately. Such involvement can be exhibited publicly today. Most spouses recognize the need for, but often do not know how to do, the essential cooperative planning that is based upon mutual respect, honesty, genuineness, and trust. Within the therapeutic atmosphere of a marriage counseling group, these needs can be expressed. In fact, many couples, obtain genuine assistance with this problem in adult education classes, marriage enrichment retreats, and in personal growth workshops that are designed for assertiveness training, contracting, cooperative planning, career planning for couples, and lifestyle planning. Couples who learn to do cooperative planning also tend to improve their communication, to express their needs more openly, to request their intimacy needs more effectively, and to form closer, more intimate relationships.

Couples who plan cooperatively have learned to sense when decisions are required, to set aside time to obtain essential information, to differentiate between facts and opinions, to define alternative solutions, to consider feelings, needs, values, and consequences of various alternatives, and to be open to alternatives. Moreover, they recognize when they have reached an impasse that requires the assistance of a trusted friend or professional who can arbitrate.

Those who have learned to do cooperative planning also recognize that it is not sufficient merely to discuss the issues, clarify them, and define alternative decisions. They must achieve a precise closure statement, e.g., "Then we have decided to postpone buying a new sofa so that we can have the car overhauled for our vacation trip." When partners fail to achieve such closure, either may assume his preferred solution, act on it, and then be shocked by his spouse's anger or disappointment. Another common problem experienced by those who discuss decisions and fail to achieve closure is decision by default. Failure to decide unknowingly becomes a decision, and often a bad one.

Some couples require more assistance than they can get from reading about cooperative decision making, hearing a brief description of the process, and using role playing within their counseling group to practice the process and obtain feedback from other clients. For them, special sessions are required

A man must make the important decisions.

What is best for my husband and his career must always be considered first.

to discuss, clarify, and practice these principles.

By scheduling special sessions for only the couples who require them, the instruction can be more effective. Moreover, the counselor tends to avoid interrupting normal therapeutic talk and portraying himself primarily as a teacher. Usually several other couples ask to observe the instruction.

Smaby and Tamminen's (1978) format for training counselors is useful for these sessions. The counselor begins by reviewing the Smaby and Tamminen format and the important aspects of cooperative planning; then he helps the couple for whom the session was planned to identify specific decisions with which they would like help and asks one of the observers to help them apply these principles in learning cooperative decision making. Usually the helper is observed as he works with the couple. Then he solicits feedback from the observer and the couple. Sometimes another couple will volunteer to demonstrate applications of these cooperative planning principles. During the course of the session every couple is given an opportunity to obtain assistance in practicing the decision-making process with a helper and observer, to serve as helper and observer, and to work alone in implementing the process on their own (and, of course, getting feedback and assistance with the problems with which they were confronted when working alone).

Requests Vs. Demands

Good communication skills are essential for a good marriage. Frequently, those who require assistance in learning cooperative planning must first learn communication skills (Gottman, Notarius, Gonso, & Markman, 1976). Usually this is begun by helping each to think about and to describe recent instances in which they encountered problems in trying to discuss a controversial issue, to resolve a conflict, and/or to do cooperative planning. These situations tend to occur when either the message sender or the receiver or both are incongruent or when one makes a request that is communicated as a demand. Once couples are taught to recognize these distinctions, they become very adept at detecting the games that other couples play in resolving conflict. They learn to help other couples review the tape recordings of sessions to pick out where either party was incongruent or one made a request that was conveyed as a demand, to help them analyze their behavior, and to use their new knowledge to "replay" scenes to demonstrate asking rather than demanding. As a consequence, they feel better because they have communicated their requests accurately.

The Power Struggle

Almost everyone at some time encounters an incident in an intimate relationship in which *she is determined to control*, perhaps not only the resolution of that particular problem, but also the other person and the relationship. Perhaps she also experiences a great need to prove that she is right. If afterwards she considers whether the power struggle was worth it, she may try to answer such questions as: Did the winner pay too big a price for winning? Why was it so important for me to prove that I was in charge—that I had the right to decide? Why was it so important for me to be right? Considering what happened and the price each party paid, what do I wish that I could have done differently? How could I have made a case for my participation in the decision-making process more assertively rather than doing it so aggressively?

When Cathy and Rolf were first married, Rolf asked her to deposit his check in his bank. In a conversation with the bank teller, whom she knew, the teller suggested that Cathy sign the appropriate forms for a joint checking account. She did it and made a note to herself to transfer her account to this bank and to talk with Rolf about finances and savings. Before she had a chance to do either, Rolf discovered what she had done and was enraged. It reminded him of his conniving, selfish mother. Moreover, he believed that the husband should handle the finances. Had they not already enrolled in a newlyweds marriage enrichment retreat in which they were helped to resolve the conflict, a real power struggle could have developed.

Most spouses have some desire to control the other—especially at the beginning of the marriage. When this desire for control is challenged, there is a tendency for a power struggle to surface—both as a defensive and offensive tactic. Neither spouse has to control. They can learn to do cooperative planning, but few have observed good models and most probably doubt that it can work. Thus, both the attitude and the skills for cooperative planning must be developed to replace the self-defeating need to control and/or to be right.

Just recognizing what a problem it can be and why it occurs is especially helpful to young couples as they begin their marriage. So does helping spouses identify those areas in their lives in which they feel that they must make decisions, especially areas of potential disagreement. Couples are encouraged to select one of these areas, reverse roles, practice making a decision on that topic, renegotiate it as themselves, and listen to feedback from other couples in the group. Then they select another decision area for homework. The observing couples tend to catch on to the role players' self-defeating, power struggle games and offer good suggestions for managing them. When they are confronted with a spouse, or even a couple, who is reluctant to give up the power struggle, they help the couple discuss the consequences of refusing to change. Moreover, it also helps for the counselor to tell a natural consequence story in which a couple who refused to do anything about a similar problem was hurt by their refusal to discuss the problem and resolve it.

Assertiveness Training

Throughout this book the point has been made that partnership of equals is essential for a good marriage. In order for partners to achieve intimacy and maintain it, each must be able to be genuine, considerate, loving, and trustful in order to enjoy each other's companionship, to communicate effectively, to make cooperative decisions, and to recognize and resolve conflicts. To do this, they must learn to be assertive with each other.

Some couples find it relatively easy to understand the difference between assertiveness and aggressiveness. They can learn the distinction through role playing the process of making a decision or resolving a conflict, using feedback from the other couples to evaluate their progress, reading about assertiveness (Cotler and Guerra, 1975; Lange and Jakubowski, 1978), and selecting other decisions and/or conflicts to practice on between sessions is sufficient. Other couples, however, need additional outside-of-counseling group assertiveness training sessions. They need to further clarify the differences between assertiveness and aggressiveness, to discuss the underlying beliefs and values that keep them from acting assertively, and to review situations in which they fail to act assertively and the kinds of people they have difficulty responding assertively to. Some persons also require assistance in recognizing and expressing the satisfactions that accrue from behaving assertively and in soliciting reinforcement from relatives, friends, and co-workers (significant others) with whom they are learning to be assertive.

Lifestyle Decisions

Clergymen and counselors should help prospective marriage partners discover and share their hopes and dreams, study and compare their lifestyles, identify the values and beliefs about which they genuinely agree and disagree, discover techniques for enjoying their differences as differences rather than as deficiencies, and negotiate problems that rise from their differences in beliefs, values, and lifestyles.

Even couples who believe that they are compatible and have similar beliefs and values are often surprised to discover, through an inventory of each one's unique preferences in lifestyle, the degree to which their lifestyle priorities differ on: time allocations alone, with each other, with friends, with family, and for work-related activities; the importance of career success; church activities and the general significance of spiritual and/or religious life; the significance of social life and social recognition; the importance of financial success and money management; the place and significance of children in each one's life; commitment to marriage, family, community improvement, and politics. Preparing the members of a couples' group to do a personal inventory of lifestyle goals, to arrange items from most important to least important, to share each one's list with his spouse, and to discuss and negotiate a common listing of priorities may produce some threatening conflicts, but it also helps them identify the issues on which they must work. They must either resolve most of their differences or learn to live with them. Values clarification exercises (Piercy & Schultz, 1978) can be used to help couples negotiate these differences. The atmosphere in the group encourages spouses to resolve their differences because they see others struggling with similar kinds of differences and resolving them.

Such discussions can be especially profitable for newly-weds. Failure to face up to the problems that result from one's partner's values and lifestyle differences creates difficulties that continue to plague even a couple whose marriage has survived years of conflict. Such discomfort can be prevented if such people recognize before marriage that they have irreconcilable differences. For these people the best alternative is not marrying or getting professional help prior to their marriage or in its early years.

Cooperative Career Planning

When a counselor discovers that couples require assistance in cooperative career planning, he encourages each spouse to review his own career plan by independently doing the following: (1) try to recall the first time he can remember thinking about what he would like to do when he seeks full-time employment; (2) note with whom he shared these plans and how that person or persons reacted; (3) recall whether he considered any alternative careers; (4) record his answers to the previous questions for every choice between the time of his first choice and the present; (5) consider whether or not he would like to change careers now, and if so, what his choice would be; (6) evaluate his chances for getting into a training program, completing it, and obtaining employment; determine whether he needs additional information to answer any of these questions for which he requires new data about either himself or the job opportunities; (7) decide what he would try next if he should discover that he cannot implement his choice; (8) think of whose assistance he will require to achieve either of these goals; (9) define his dream goal, decide whether or not it is realistic, and decide what he is going to do about it; and (10) determine how his spouse fits into his career plan and the extent to which she has participated in its development.

Some clients require extensive assistance in learning to do cooperative career planning. Usually some of the other clients in their counseling group ask to observe them in the process or to participate with them. Others may be invited by the counselor to assist him in teaching the process and to model the process with role playing. Participants in the special cooperative career planning session are given a sheet that includes the ten career-related questions just listed, suggestions that will help clients answer those questions, and suggestions for initiating discussions about those plans. Following the discussion of the questions, clients are encouraged to think about and report back on their private discussions of these questions: Do both of you plan to work full-time? How can you help each other develop a support system for coping with problems at work and/or the problems that result from both working? If one is going to work outside the home for the first time, what must be done to renegotiate home management or child-rearing duties? If the husband is offered an unusual promotion, is it appropriate for him to ask his wife to give up her position and relocate? If the wife is offered an unusual promotion, is it appropriate for her to ask her husband to give up his position and relocate?

Some couples who have the same careers are trying to share positions—each working from half to three-quarters of the time and sharing home and child-rearing responsibilities. Though this proposal makes sense and some couples have been able to do it, it has been very difficult. Employers tend to deprive both spouses of certain fringe benefits that they provide for full-time employees.

Since these couples have already discussed the problem that they have in cooperative planning, have practiced their new planning skills, and have dealt with their lifestyle differences, they usually have developed the skills that they need to do cooperative planning. Yet it is still difficult—especially when both are ambitious, independent adults—to make it work. They must be highly motivated to be considerate of the other's career development, to exhibit commitment to resolve conflicts that result from promotions, and to learn to provide support for each other when confronted with both work-related and home management problems.

Contracting

Successful marriage partners have learned to talk things out and to plan cooperatively. They realize that they can expect to be confronted with new problems and that at different stages in their lives they will have to review their expectations of each other, confirm those on which they still agree, and reach new agreements on new issues. They have learned to recognize and to cope with passages, and they are committed to work on developing an ever-growing relationship.

Still, while most couples agree on certain things, there often are unresolved and undiscussed issues that are potentially fraught with danger.

> It is generally recognized that most married couples have mutually agreed upon purposes and goals—for example, raising healthy children, living frugally in order to save money to retire in Florida, or establishing a reputation as solid citizens in the community. But it is often overlooked that goal achievement involves a highly complicated and sometimes incompatible or antithetical use of time and energy. . . .
>
> In a functional marriage, the spouses have agreed upon rules of the relationship—that they will discuss hurt feelings or misunderstandings, that they will circulate at parties, and so on. They have discussed who will do what when. Here again we see the importance of mutual agreement (after negotiation) concerning most aspects of marriage. Unilateral autonomy is almost always dangerous to a marriage because it implies rejection, abandonment, or inequality. The spouses must be in accord about most of the behaviors of each, and compromises must be made. The firm hands of quid pro quo are always at the steering wheel of the workable marriage. When there is no agreement about where it is going, the marriage is almost certain to run into a ditch (Lederer & Jackson, 1968, pp. 174, 197).

Sometimes people cannot resolve their disagreements informally. When this happens, a formal contract can help. Sager (1976) describes how the process of contracting evolves:

> The central concept is that each partner in a marriage brings to it an individual, unwritten contract, a set of expectations and promises, conscious and unconscious. These individual contracts may be modified during marriage but will remain separate unless the two partners are fortunate enough to arrive at a single joint contract which is "felt" and agreed to at all levels

of awareness, or unless they work toward a single contract with professional help. . . .

The contracts that contemporary couples sign together usually include the following provisions: (1) division of household labor; (2) use of living space; (3) each partner's responsibility for child rearing and socialization; (4) property, debts, living expenses; (5) career commitment and legal domicile; (6) rights of inheritance; (7) use of surnames; (8) range of permissible relationships with others; (9) obligations of the marital dyad in various life sectors such as work, leisure, and community and social life; (10) grounds for splitting or divorce; (11) initial and subsequent contract periods and negotiability; (12) sexual fidelity/relationships beyond partnerships; and (13) position regarding procreation or adoption of children. . . .

Ideally each person's contract should be consistent within itself and congruent with or complimentary to the partner's contract. Contracts that approach this ideal evolve into a single effective contract that both spouses subscribe to consciously and freely. It is not necessary or even desirable for all terms to be identical, so long as the partners know where differences prevent serious disharmony or dissatisfaction. When dissatisfaction does occur, as it inevitably will, mates must be able to express themselves and their feelings, communicate well, and verbally fight through differences to some equitable solution (pp. ix–x, 2, 104).

From the outset, the counselor can emphasize the two separate kinds of contracts. This distinction enables him to identify particular sources of trouble within the marriage rather early and to begin working out a likely contract that will address the couple's interactional concerns. This approach allows him to avoid becoming mired in the incomprehensible complaints and countercomplaints that often leave both spouses exhausted on the "battlefield" while the therapist feels as helpless as a UN peacekeeping observer. Other couples tend to recognize such unproductive "war games" and often redirect the couple's attention to more constructive topics (Sager, 1976).

The counselor usually introduces the process by providing couples with the basic skills required for contracting: (1) by helping them identify the primary issues on which they must learn to do cooperative planning at present, teaching them the process itself, and using role playing to practice the process in their counseling group (and often with role-reversal role playing between counseling sessions); (2) by teaching them and giving them an opportunity to practice new assertive behaviors; and (3) by teaching them how to recognize and cope with the underlying feelings and needs that precipitate their power struggles. Then he invites the couples in the group to list the items on which they believe the couple must develop contractual agreements. Then he asks the other clients to supplement their lists with any additional ones that they may have omitted. After each couple has agreed on the items for which they require agreements, each is asked to write out a preferred contract on those items. They are encouraged to be as specific as possible and to use language that will enable them to determine the extent to which they are living up to their own proposed agreements. When this has been done, the counselor asks one couple to volunteer to demonstrate for the others how to apply their new cooperative planning and assertive training skills in negotiating their contract—first by reversing roles and then by replaying the scene in his own role in negotiating the contract. Usually this experience produces much discussion material and prepares other couples to begin their negotiations.

For many people this is sufficient. Again, some will require so much additional training and time that the counseling group may prefer to have them either obtain that help from the counselor between regular counseling sessions or to join a special training session or workshop for that purpose.

Summary

Cooperative decision making is the cornerstone of successful contemporary marriages. In order to master and implement cooperative planning, partners must respect each other, set aside time to find out what the other thinks and feels, differentiate between facts and opinions, be able to define and evaluate alternative decisions, consider each other's feelings, needs, and values, and achieve closure on decisions. After couples have learned cooperative planning, assertive behaviors, to make requests rather than demands, and to recognize and manage power struggles, they are ready to learn to do contracting.

Questions to Think About

1. Mace and Mace (1978) have concluded that the following ten items are crucial for a successful marriage: common goals and values, commitment to growth, communication skills, creative use of conflict, appreciation and affection, agreement on gender roles, cooperation and team work, sexual fulfillment, money management, and parent effectiveness. You and your spouse are asked to rank these in terms of each one's priority of importance. After you have ranked them independently, use your individual rankings to develop a couple's ranking. With what problems were you confronted in achieving a common list? What new items would you each like to add to the list? Could you agree where to place the new items?
2. With what problems are you and your spouse confronted when attempting to plan cooperatively?
3. Differentiate between hostile behavior and aggressive behavior.
4. Differentiate between aggressive behavior and assertive behavior.
5. What are the crucial elements for a counselor to remember in helping a couple learn: (a) to do cooperative planning; (b) to cope with the power struggle; (c) to request intimacy; (d) to make requests; (e) to develop a marriage contract and revise it.

References

Cotler, S. B., & Guerra, J. J. *Assertion training: A humanistic-behavioral guide to self-dignity.* Champaign, Ill.: Research Press, 1975.

Gottman, J., Notarius, C., Gonso, J., & Markman, H. *A couple's guide to communication.* Champaign, Ill.: Research Press, 1976.

Lange, A. J., & Jakubowski, P. *Responsible assertive behavior:*

Cognitive/behavioral procedures for trainers. Champaign, Ill.: Research Press, 1978.

Lederer, W. J., & Jackson, D. D. *The mirages of marriage.* New York: W. W. Norton, 1968.

Mace, D. R., & Mace, V. C. Measure your marriage potential: A simple test that tells couples where they are. *The Family Coordinator,* 1978, *27,* 63–67.

Piercy, F., & Schultz, K. Values clarification strategies for couples enrichment. *The Family Coordinator,* 1978, *27,* 175–178.

Sager, C. J. *Marriage contracts and couple therapy.* New York: Brunner-Mazel, 1976.

Smaby, M. H., & Tamminen, A. W. Counseling for decisions. *Personnel and Guidance Journal,* 1978, *57,* 106–110.

11

MANAGING CONFLICT

Conflicts are an inevitable, integral, and inescapable part of a meaningful marital relationship. Spouses who cannot accept conflict as a normal phenomenon and commit themselves to admitting and resolving their conflicts can expect their marriage to last only as long as they can deceive themselves and suppress their differences (Mace & Mace, 1977).

Furthermore, Lerner (1964) learned something that appears to be highly relevant for married partners who have children. When he compared conflict resolution behaviors of parents of hospitalized normal and emotionally disturbed adolescents, he discovered that a significantly greater number of normal youths came from families in which conflict was faced and resolved, whereas a significantly greater number of disturbed youths came from families in which conflict was ignored and denied.

Conflict Vs. Anger

Conflict is disagreement. It is a condition that may result from opposing plans, differences in lifestyles, and expectations that were never clear and mutually agreed upon. It may also occur when couples fail to agree on how to express and manage anger.

Anger is a common response to all conflict. Anger is a strong, negative feeling that may be expressed in very different ways, ranging from a defensive coverup for a guilt response to fear or revenge.

Some people find it impossible to distinguish conflict from anger. Yet, while conflict and anger are not mutually exclusive, they needn't go hand in hand, and anger needn't dominate every conflict or disagreement. Couples who learn to manage conflict tend to substitute productive responses to conflict in place of their anger.

When a couple has a conflict and the counselor is not sure how much unexpressed anger the spouses have suppressed, it usually is productive if the counselor tries to develop an accurate reflection that will expose both spouses' true feelings. (Of course, he encourages other members of the group to do the same.)This approach reflects a basic counseling procedure that has been stressed throughout this book: clients should be helped to recognize and considerately express their own genuine feelings so that they can recognize their own pain, define their own treatment goals, accept responsibility for their own growth, and solicit their spouse's reinforcement to accomplish these ends. Couples who succeed at managing conflict enrich their lives immeasurably.

> You can't be loving when you are angry, and you can't be angry when you are loving—the two exclude each other. But you can't be continuously loving, either, when the threat of possible anger hangs over you—however remote the threat may be. Only when you have brought anger under control in your marriage—and we mean by accepting and resolving it

If you had the guts to ask for the raise that you deserve, we wouldn't be in this financial bind.

If you'd forgo some of your unnecessary expenditures, we could accumulate some savings, and I wouldn't have to beg for a raise.

together, not by suppressing it—does the way lie clear and open to a continuing growth in love and intimacy. . . .

The couples who give up and miss out don't realize that the happiness they were seeking is really there, but it can be realized only when they work right through the conflict, instead of evading it. If they only knew how to do this to the point of resolution, they would strengthen their relationship instead of weakening it. But they don't know this, because the culture doesn't tell them that the conflicts in marriage are really growth points in their relationship, and that the creative use of conflict is the golden key that opens the door to lasting happiness (Mace & Mace, 1977, pp. 115, 105).

Causes

There are several sources of conflict between married couples:
1. The failure of couples to discuss and reach specific agreements on what they may expect from each other regarding such things as household duties, financial management, child rearing, and the degree of involvement with in-laws
2. The failure to fulfill agreed-upon commitments and agree on what is satisfactory performance for each
3. The clash of values and/or differences in lifestyle
4. The perception of differences as faults rather than as differences in values and/or lifestyles
5. The use of complaints and/or demands instead of requests
6. The failure to discuss and develop shared marriage goals
7. The failure to discuss and develop agreements on basic items in their marriage contract and to review these periodically and, when appropriate, revise them
8. The failure to achieve intimacy goals
9. Jealousy (resulting either from a couple's failure to agree on the degree of intimate relationships outside marriage or from the spouse who is the "hunter" being bored with the marital relationship)
10. Sexual dysfunctioning
11. The failure to achieve closure in a decision or the failure of

the spouses to communicate what they thought that they
agreed to
12. Inadequate preparation for crises and passages

Of all the reasons for conflict listed above, some believe
that jealousy is the most difficult to manage. Individuals who
feel this way do not seem to realize that jealousy is a signal that
is telling them to attend to themselves and the particular relationship (Clanton & Smith, 1977b). Jealousy is threatening for
most people to admit and to deal with, but it can be done by
owning and communicating one's genuine feelings—especially in a marriage counseling group in which the individual will
receive genuine support. Group support usually is readily
available and accessible for one simple reason: just about
everyone in the group has experienced jealousy to a greater or
lesser degree.

> Tell your partner what kinds of behavior and what
> kind of people are most likely to trigger your jealousy,
> and get your partner to tell you the same. Talk about
> what you would do in various hypothetical situations.
> Find out what your partner expects of you, and make
> sure he or she knows what your expectations are. Be
> willing to negotiate new limits. Discuss particular per-
> sons and situations but don't limit yourself to that.
> Discuss your needs and limits, your beliefs and
> values. Seek congruence, but don't be upset if you
> discover discrepancies.
>
> As long as human beings need affection, there
> will be some jealousy. It probably cannot be com-
> pletely eradicated. Even if you are relatively success-
> ful in working with your jealousy it will most likely
> recur in some form at some time. Don't be surprised
> when this happens. The jealous flash is a perfectly
> natural response. You'll feel it every time an important
> relationship appears to be threatened. Your jealousy
> is neither proof of love nor evidence of personal fail-
> ure. It is merely a signal which tells you to attend to
> your relationship and to yourself (Clanton & Smith,
> 1977a, p. 82).

Most of the causes listed previously call for the development of cooperative planning skills (see Chapter 10). While the

group will help an individual couple learn to plan cooperatively, the couple, in turn, will help the group. To the degree
that the couple succeeds in learning new behaviors and
modeling them effectively, other group members will be encouraged to do the same.

On Fighting

As was said earlier in this chapter, couples must learn to
recognize signs that suggest anger and manage it. They also
must learn to fight fairly. Bach and Wyden (1968) teach couples
to fight fairly. The conflict that they helped Lisa and Tim Con-
don resolve illustrates how, in addition to learning the principles of fighting, couples can help each other resolve specific
conflicts. The Condons' ritual was mutual punishment for feeling unlovable. She felt unloved because he was stingy. He felt
unloved because she punished him by spending more money
than he had.

> First, we advised them to declare a moratorium and
> engage in no money fight unless they used it to intro-
> duce fresh information on how they really felt about
> this issue.
>   Second, we asked them to introduce a specific
> change so that the exact situation that led to their last
> money fight couldn't occur again. Tom thereupon
> opened a separate checking account for Lisa.
>   Third, we asked them to flush out, with the help of
> fight techniques to be discussed here, the real issues
> behind their round robins. In the case of the Condons,
> mutual probing brought out that Lisa felt bad because
> Tom wouldn't ask for a raise at the office; Tom resented
> that Lisa wouldn't help accumulate cash toward emer-
> gencies (p. 58).

These techniques work best in marriage counseling
groups because other couples can help the fighting couple by
exposing their self-defeating behaviors and encouraging them
to identify and practice more constructive alternatives.

Obviously, Bach and Wyden's approach requires that
couples be motivated, patient, good willed, flexible, and willing to experiment with new and challenging ways of resolving

their problems. As difficult as this may be, most of their clients who have approached their conflict in this way fight fairly rather quickly. And the payoffs for doing so have been very rewarding:

> Since they live fewer lies and inhibitions and have discarded outmoded notions of etiquette, these couples are free to grow emotionally, to become more productive and more creative as individuals in their own right and also as pairs. Their sex lives tend to improve. They are likely to do a better job raising their children. They feel less guilty about hostile emotions that they harbor against each other. Their communications improve and, as a result, they face fewer unpleasant surprises from partners. Our graduates know how to make the here-and-now more livable for themselves, and so they worry much less about the past that cannot be changed. They are less likely to become victims of boredom or divorce. They feel less vulnerable and more loving toward each other because they are protected by an umbrella of reasonable standards for what is fair and foul in their relationship. Perhaps best of all they are liberated to be themselves (pp. 17–18).

Early Discovery and Management

Rarely does it do any good to try to help disagreeing parties prove who was at fault. Sometimes, however, one spouse persists in trying to establish blame to look good in the eyes of other group members and, perhaps, to get revenge. When the counselor discovers a strong need for revenge, he should reflect this need and, possibly, use the idea of the natural consequence story (based upon a real occurrence but changed sufficiently to keep confidences) to facilitate discussion of the natural consequences of vengeful behavior. The case he selects should contain many common elements with the present client's case.

Frank's case illustrates how the counselor uses this strategy. Even though Ruth had made several attempts to enlist Frank's assistance in resolving the problem that arose at a

cocktail party when Frank felt that Ruth reacted very seduc-
tively to his boss, Frank continued to try to prove how bad Ruth
was. The counselor said, "Frank, you remind me of a fellow
named Fred I used to know. He often complained about his
wife's seductive behavior, but he refused to help her resolve
their problems. Eventually she got fed up with his putdowns,
found a really nice guy, divorced him, and married the other
guy." The counselor's comment precipitated considerable discussion in the counseling group as such a natural consequence
story usually does. It also encouraged Frank to stop nagging
Ruth and to ask her to help him cope with his jealousy.

Confronted by a couple in conflict, what can a friend or
counselor or even a counseling group do to help them resolve
their conflict? First, the helper must give each partner a chance
to discuss the problem as he perceives it. As one partner talks,
the helper must help the other partner to listen as a helper
rather than as a combatant, to try to empathize with her
spouse, and to try to help her spouse identify the crucial issues
in this particular conflict. (In other words, apply the triad model
described in Chapter 1.) During each partner's discussion of the
problem, the helper listens for underlying pain and clues that
reveal each partner's motivation (or lack of motivation) to
change, formulates reflections to uncover and encourage discussion of pain and motivation to change, and helps each to
decide what new behaviors she must learn to become increasingly the kind of person that she would like to become.

When this process occurs during a group session, it is often
profitable for the counselor to pause and invite the entire group
to help the couple answer the following questions:
1. In *this particular conflict*, what is the problem as each of
   you perceive it?
2. What are the issues? Which of your own particular needs,
   values, or beliefs are involved?
3. What compromises are essential to resolve it?
4. Can you negotiate the essential compromises by your-
   selves or do you require someone else's assistance to negotiate them?
5. Whose cooperation is required to resolve this conflict and
   implement the solution? Whose cooperation is required to
   help you discover what you have learned in resolving this
   conflict and apply these learnings in new situations?

6. How may you solicit this assistance? Who will contact each helper or helpers?
7. What new behaviors must each of you learn to improve your conflict management skills?
8. What must each of you do to reinforce your spouse's conflict management skills?
9. What criteria can each of you use to appraise your success in improving your conflict management skills?
10. What can you do to celebrate your successes in improving your conflict management skills?

Since question 1 has usually been answered by both spouses the first time the counselor attempts to teach conflict resolution, the counselor often finds it profitable to begin the discussion of the questions presented above with directions such as,

> Now you have an idea how we can use the questions that we have listed on the blackboard to help Frank and Ruth resolve this particular conflict. Instead of having Frank speak again for himself and Ruth speak for herself in answering the first question, I'd like to suggest that Frank take Ruth's role and Ruth take Frank's role and use role playing to show us how the conflict developed. Then let each speak for his spouse in answering the first question. After they have done that and have obtained feedback from each other and us and after we have analyzed the role playing, then we will have each partner be himself and help them discuss the other questions.

Finally, the members help the couple decide what decisions they must make, what help they require in making these decisions, what new behaviors each must learn, where these new behaviors can be introduced and practiced, and why they will report back to the group, e.g., to celebrate their successes, to develop new strategies, to cope with alternatives that didn't work, and/or to seek encouragement and reinforcement.

In the early stages of learning to manage conflict, marriage partners should be encouraged to improve their skills in identifying early clues that suggest irritation, anger, or disappointment and to discuss these feelings before hurtful, unproductive conflicts and/or fights develop. Each also must learn to help his partner differentiate between guilt-induced anger and anger that results from the other's inconsiderate behavior. When it is the former, his mate must help him discuss what he does not like about himself and/or his disappointing behavior and decide precisely how he wants to learn to behave differently, including learning to accept his imperfect self. When it is the latter, he must learn to face his spouse, tell her precisely how he was hurt by her behavior, and request her help in resolving their conflict.

Summary

Conflicts are inevitable in marital relationships. Those who have successful marriages learn to recognize the early symptoms of conflict, develop essential conflict management skills, learn from their conflicts, encourage each other to deal directly with their disagreements, and exhibit essential commitment for enriching their relationships. Facing conflict and seeking constructive alternatives to uncontrolled expression of anger will strengthen a marital relationship.

Questions to Think About

1. What are the implications of Lerner's findings for improving human relationships in families?
2. How does learning to manage conflict enrich marriage partners' relationships? Recall from your own personal experiences specific instances in which conflicts have been well managed and very poorly managed. Recall the impact of each on you.
3. Why is jealousy such a serious problem for married couples? What must they do to resolve it?
4. Which of the common causes for conflict are most difficult for you to manage? Which call for your mastery of new human relations skills?

References

Bach, G. R., & Wyden, P. *The intimate enemy.* New York: Avon, 1968.

Clanton, G., & Smith, L. The self-inflicted pain of jealousy. *Psychology Today,* 1977a, *10,* 44–47, 80, 82.

———. *Jealousy.* Englewood Cliffs, N.J.: Prentice Hall, 1977b.

Lerner, P. M. *Resolution of intrafamilial conflict in families of schizophrenic patients.* Unpublished doctoral dissertation, University of Illinois, 1964.

Mace, D. R., & Mace, V. *How to have a happy marriage.* Nashville, Tenn.: Parthenon Press, 1977.

12

PARENTING GROUPS

Parenting groups are designed to help people discover and apply strategies for coping with the child-rearing problems they confront. Though a greater number of participants tend to be mothers, the counselor should try very hard to schedule the sessions when both parents can attend. Fathers as well as mothers require assistance in encouraging the emotional, intellectual, moral, and social development of their children, and when both parents participate, the chances of developing the kind of nurturing home atmosphere described in Chapter 9 are likewise increased. Even when most mothers were full-time homemakers, the full partnership of fathers was needed for most effective child rearing. When either parent shirks his responsibility for rearing his children, the children suffer.

Faced with a marked increase in children's behavior and learning problems in schools, child abuse and neglect, and juvenile delinquency, society is beginning to give more attention to child-rearing practices. Perhaps this has made even the parents of normal children realize more fully how difficult child rearing is. It requires the best efforts of cooperating partners who can discuss the problems they face in rearing their children and reach a common understanding on a variety of questions. What should they expect of their children? How can they support each other by reinforcing desired child-rearing behaviors? What can they do to enrich their family life? What are the best strategies for coping with specific problems? How can they encourage their children to participate in solving the family's problems and in improving the quality of family life? During the course of these discussion groups, many counselors show couples how to introduce and maintain a family council as a way of encouraging children's participation in the development and maintenance of a wholesome family life (Dreikurs, 1972a; Dreikurs, 1972b; Dreikurs, Gould, & Corsini, 1974).

Parenting groups have much in common with marriage counseling groups. Participants share their problems and learn specific new behaviors to replace certain self-defeating ones. They learn to be good helpers as well as good clients. Role-playing techniques are used frequently in both groups. The triad model is used to help spouses substitute each other's helping responses for complaining, countercomplaining, and nagging. Spouses also are taught cooperative planning and partnership skills.

Yet there are important differences. Whereas marriage counseling clients learn to manage the most private elements of their own lives, participants in parenting groups for the most part only discuss family-related issues: learning to manage their children and to develop the kind of family atmosphere that nurtures wholesome development of children (see Chapter 9). Usually the leader assumes more of a teaching role than when counseling spouses. She teaches parents to identify early symptoms that suggest social, emotional, and learning prob-

lems, to define the desired child behaviors they wish to reinforce, to identify specific ways of reinforcing these desired behaviors, and to work together as partners in helping each other master these skills. She provides them with materials to read on child-rearing practices and teaches them how to solicit help from other participants in implementing the ideas that they select to apply. She also teaches them how to identify and use community resources, to develop a support group, and to introduce and maintain a family council.

Some churches and community outreach programs in regional mental health centers have developed good parenting centers to supplement their parenting groups. In addition, Adlerian family education centers (Dreikurs, 1972a) have sprung up all around the country to provide continuing services for families. When a family seeks assistance at such a center, they are encouraged to bring their children with them. Usually the leader first interviews the parents, then the children, and finally interviews them together in the presence of the observing families. Using this process, the counselor learns what individual members of the family perceive to be the major family problems and enlists the other family members' assistance in deciding what each family member can do to alleviate their problems. Where any or most of the members exhibit little or no interest in doing anything to correct their difficulties, the leader helps the family explore the consequences of their inaction. In general, she tries to help participants learn to increase their encouraging behaviors and to decrease their discouraging behaviors. At the close of the session with a family, she encourages the observers, the other families who are present for the session, to ask questions of individual members of the family and to react to proposed actions, to suggest alternatives, and to encourage members to implement the desired new behaviors that were discussed. Observers also share their successes in handling similar problems within their families.

The Presentation

The presentation used to introduce parenting groups to prospective participants is basically the same as for marriage groups. Besides describing what usually occurs in such groups, the leader describes the texts used (Becker, 1971; Dreikurs & Soltz, 1964; Ginott, 1965; Gordon, 1970) and suggests where they can be purchased and how they can be used most advantageously. K. A. Clark-Stewart (1978) reviews commonly used materials.

Usually best results are obtained from a presentation when the counselor describes the helping process for prospective participants and answers their questions about himself and his techniques for helping them. Sometimes for community outreach programs and adult education programs he is required to provide a brief written description (preferably no longer than a double-spaced typewritten page) that is published in the agency's house organ for constituents. When this is done, the leader should designate a time and place where prospective participants can meet him to evaluate him and to get their questions concerning expectations answered. When he is going to be presented to a group that is meeting for another purpose, he should brief the person who introduces him so that they cover essential information in two or three minutes. The presentation below was made by the pastor who knew about the process from his church's previous participation in the program.

> By now most of you who are parents have discovered that child rearing is one of your most challenging responsibilities, and perhaps the one for which you were least prepared. Personally, I have found parenting groups to be very helpful, and I am pleased that we can offer them to our members and their friends.
>
> Dr. Thompson, a member of our church and a psychologist whom most of you know, will be conducting a parenting discussion group for couples. These discussion groups are designed to provide a forum in which couples with children of approximately the same age can share ideas on child rearing, discuss strategies for coping with problems, and get help in putting these strategies into practice.
>
> The groups will meet for an hour and a half once a week for six to eight weeks. Those who are interested should meet with Dr. Thompson in the lounge after this service to get answers to your questions about the sessions, to obtain a more complete written description of the group process, and more information on the

texts to be used. We would also appreciate it if those interested in participating would complete a card on which you report your names, telephone numbers, your preferred meeting time, and the age of the child with which you'd most like assistance.

The Group Process

Prior to the first meeting, clients are expected to skim the suggested texts, discuss them, and purchase the one they like best and feel is most congruent with their lifestyle. After they have decided on a text and purchased it, they are expected to read it independently. As a client reads, she should note specific child-rearing problems with which she would like help, the techniques that she feels would help her cope with her problems, and share her list of goals with her spouse. When they have identified the new techniques, they should begin talking about how each can help the other to implement desired new behaviors and to identify those with which they would like assistance from the group. In other words, the discussions focus on helping individuals implement the new ideas they learn from the books and each other. Participants also learn to be more open in discussing child-rearing problems, to detect their child-rearing frustrations, fears, and dreams, and to listen better to each other rather than to complain and belittle each other for past failures. Furthermore, they feel more normal when they discover that other normal parents have similar problems that they are learning to solve—that within such a supporting group they can learn the desired new behaviors that are essential in order to facilitate the normal development of their children. They also learn to more effectively express their positive feelings to each other and to their children and to reinforce their children's desirable behaviors.

Participants can profit from discussing several other questions as well: What should we know about our child's development? With what developmental tasks may each child be confronted? How can we assess whether or not our child is making normal career, emotional, intellectual, moral, physical, or social growth? What can we do to enhance his development in each of these areas? What behaviors and/or reactions suggest our child's need for remedial treatment for academic, moral, or emotional development? What do we have the right to expect from each child? What does he have the right to expect from us? How can we enlist his assistance in developing a wholesome family atmosphere? What can we do to facilitate our child's acceptance of our moral, religious, or political values?

* Simon, Howe, and Kirshenbaum (1972) contend that every decision we make and everything we do is influenced by our beliefs, attitudes, and values and that, therefore, we must try to know what they are and how they affect our lives. Piercy and Schultz (1978) describe values clarification exercises which they have used effectively in marriage counseling groups. These exercises can be used effectively with parenting groups also. They are especially helpful in aiding parents who are struggling with several of the questions just listed.

In one group for parents of middle-school students, a couple presented the problem they were having with their bright, eighth-grade son: they were discussing improvement of his grades and encouraging him to begin exploring career choices. Though he had very good academic skills, was well-behaved, and read widely, he earned only average grades. Teaching the parents how to use value clarification exercises with him helped both him and his parents to get in touch with their differences in lifestyle and encouraged him to explore the future consequences of his present academic performance. Then the counselor met with the three of them and taught the boy to use the Fiddler Game (see Chapter 6) to decide whether to continue his extensive and varied reading or to cut back on it somewhat in order to improve his grades. Both helped, but neither motivated a real change until he selected a tentative career goal and four alternative goals. All required markedly improved academic performance. Then he decided to work out a better balance between reading what he pleased and improving his school grades.

Parents Without Partners

Nearly half of the children in this country are raised in homes that have only one parent. There are many reasons for this figure. Of course, the high divorce rate is one. Many people marry, have children, and decide that they cannot live together. In other cases, a marriage partner dies. In still other instances, an increasing number of single people have or adopt children because they want to have children but do not want to marry.

Regardless of the reason there is a sizable number of single parents, and while single parenthood has its own rewards, it also poses special problems. Such parents often profit from discussion groups for parents without partners. Some also recognize the advantages of the extended family. Lifton and Tavantzis (1979) describe a technique for helping such persons develop a supportive family structure. In addition to child-rearing problems that other parents face, single parents must contend with several common problems, such as home management, child care, sharing child care, and negotiating differences with the former spouse and his family, grieving for a deceased or divorced spouse, and learning to live without an adult partner. Some singles find that they can face and adequately cope with these problems on their own. Others, however, can't, but they can manage better with the help of a parents' discussion group.

Family Council

Some of the best work on using family councils has been done by Adlerian psychologists. Rudolf Dreikurs and his students have provided the primary leadership for the use of this technique in this country (Dreikurs, Gould, & Corsini, 1974).

This technique provides each member of the family with the opportunity to describe the problems about which he is concerned and to ask other family members to help solve the problems, to share ideas, to clarify his expectations of others, to review and modify expectations, and in general to participate in making one's family the kind of nurturing group that members desire. When, for example, a family quarrel develops over whose favorite TV program will be watched, it can be solved best by the family altogether: "This is a family problem and must be solved by the family all together. The question becomes, 'What are we going to do about it?' not Mother or Daddy saying, 'What must I do to regulate watching television?'" (Dreikurs & Soltz, 1964, p. 287).

The family council is, actually, a rather simple, common-sense concept. Since the family is supposed to be a unit, decisions that affect its members are made by the family as a unit or group. When a family decides to establish a council, they should set aside a definite hour on a definite day of each week for a meeting. This time should become a part of family routine and should not be changed unless everyone agrees. Every member should be expected to be present, and if someone decides not to attend, she still is bound by the group's decisions. This requirement, of course, encourages everyone to be present so that she can express her opinion.

Leadership of the council should be rotated so that no one can "boss" the meetings, and the chairperson must be sure that everyone has a chance to be heard. Everyone seeks solutions to particular problems, and the majority opinion rules. If parents see a course of action is going to be uncomfortable, they still must abide by it, bear the discomfort, and allow the natural results to take place. Decisions remain in force for a week, and they cannot be discussed again until the following meeting. The children learn more from these experiences than they will ever learn from words or parental impositions (Dreikurs & Soltz, 1964, pp. 301–303).

Summary

It is a part of the conventional wisdom that it is more difficult to raise children than ever before. In recent years much more attention has been paid to problems related to child rearing. Community mental health centers, adult education classes, church groups, parents without partners, and other sources of help all provide a wide range of support for parents who are struggling with child-rearing problems. Sometimes the recognition of an existing problem makes that problem seem even worse than it is. However, even the skeptics who would prefer to deny that child rearing is more difficult than it was in the past and that there is any real need for improved child-rearing techniques cannot ignore the findings reported by the media concerning increased school problems, child abuse and neglect, and juvenile delinquency. Yet, even if these problems are comparatively greater, the possible sources of help are also more numerous than ever. Parents can choose from a wide range of parenting groups that can help them learn new child-rearing strategies from books and from other parents. Parents can learn special techniques, such as role playing, family council, and the triad, to deal with their problems with their children and thereby strengthen the family unit.

Questions to Think About

1. How do parenting groups differ from marriage counseling groups for couples?
2. What special knowledge and skills do you think that the leader of a parenting group must have? How would these qualifications differ from the counselor of a marriage counseling group?
3. How can parents determine what they have a right to expect from their children morally and spiritually—intellectually—financially—politically?
4. What is the family council? How could you use it to help your family develop into a warmer, more intimate, nurturing group?
5. What did you discover that was unique about Adlerian family education centers? Where could you learn more about them?
6. What did you discover about parenting groups that would lead you to encourage your spouse to join such a group with you? What threatened you when you thought about joining such a group?
7. What else would you like to have known about parenting groups?
8. Which of the principles outlined in Chapter 11 for helping couples manage conflict could you and your spouse use to improve your family council?

References

Becker, W. C. *Parents are teachers: A child management program*. Champaign, Ill.: Research Press, 1971.

Clark-Stewart, K. A. Popular primers for parents. *American Psychologist*, 1978, 54, 389–391.

Dreikurs, R. Family counseling. *Journal of Individual Psychology*, 1972a, 23, 207–222.

———. *The challenge of child training*. New York: Hawthorne, 1972b.

Dreikurs, R., Gould, S., & Corsini, R. *Family council: The Dreikurs technique for putting an end to the war between parents and children.* Chicago: Henry Regnery, 1974.

Dreikurs, R., & Soltz, V. *Children: A challenge.* New York: Duell, Sloan and Pierce, 1964.

Ginott, H. G. *Between parent and child.* New York: Macmillan, 1965.

Gordon, T. *Parent effectiveness training.* New York: Peter Wyden Press, 1970.

Lifton, W. M., & Tavantzis, T. N. Facilitating surrogate families. *Journal for Specialists in Group Work,* 1979, *4,* 104–109.

Piercy, F., & Schultz, K. Values clarification strategies for couples enrichment. *The Family Coordinator,* 1978, *27,* 175–178.

Simon, S. B., Howe, L. W., & Kirshenbaum, H. *Values clarification: A handbook of strategies for teachers and students.* New York: Hart Publishing Company, 1972.

13

TERMINATION TECHNIQUES WITH COUPLES' GROUPS

Just as getting the group off to a good start is important, so is closing on a productive note. This means that at the end of every session, each client must understand precisely what he has agreed to do between sessions, possess the necessary skills to actually do it, be committed to doing it, and know how to ask his spouse for help and support he will need. When clients terminate counseling, they must realize what they have accomplished, what they have left to do, from whom they may obtain any additional help they require, and how they can achieve closure for the counseling relationships. When clients fail to achieve closure, they are left with unfinished business. Even those who have achieved substantial growth have their gains blunted.

Bringing a Session to a Close

Most clients appreciate a clear-cut beginning and end to a session. They want a clear signal, e.g., clients begin therapeutic talk when the counselor sits and stop when he stands up. Some clients have not learned to say their good-byes and to thank other clients for especially helpful behavior. A prompt, clearly defined closure enables the counselor to help such clients. The counselor also must set aside time occasionally to clarify group norms and homework assignments. Normally, the counselor clarifies homework assignments when they are given during the counseling sessions, but sometimes the counselor begins to wonder whether a particular client really understands what he agreed to do, whether he knows whose help to request in doing it, or whether he needs to role play a scene to develop the skills for carrying out the assignment. As closing time approaches, the counselor must allocate time for some of these activities.

Clients should be encouraged to work at full speed for the entire counseling session. However, prior to the close of the first session, the counselor must check to determine whether clients understand what is expected of them just before they complete the session. Closing activities should be kept to the bare essentials. Consequently, few counselors summarize at the end of a session anymore. A few encourage a client to volunteer to summarize accomplishments and assignments for the group.

Some resisting clients reveal a lot of painful material just before the close of a session in order to protect themselves from dealing with it fully or to manipulate the group into extending the session and thereby expressing special caring for them. The counselor must deal with such clients promptly. They should be given a choice: either the counselor schedules an extra session with the couple in order to help the resisting client practice discussing the painful material and develop appropriate goals for dealing with it at the beginning of the next session, or the client begins the next session discussing his need for group members to treat him specially. Both approaches encourage clients to accept responsibility for beginning the session with therapeutic talk and for continuing it throughout the session.

We learned to do most of the
things that we hoped to learn,
but I am most enthusiastic about
our sentimental touching.

The Decision to Terminate

Most counselors terminate a group whenever a majority of the clients decides that either they have achieved their goals or that they have accomplished all that they can at present. Individuals realize that they can drop out of the group whenever they choose, but most who achieve their goals early in the life of the group usually elect to continue membership in order to help others in the group achieve their goals. Consequently they also learn from others' successes and resolve new problems that they uncover during the course of helping others.

Deciding when to terminate is an important part of the treatment process. Allowing a client to remain in a group when he is being hurt or when he fails to make adequate progress is unethical and tends to lead such a client to believe that he can never be helped by anyone. Moreover, some successful groups are permitted to continue too long. In other words, even a group which has been successful may be permitted to die with dissatisfied clients when it could have been helped to terminate on a healthy note.

Whenever all or part of the group feels that the group has fulfilled its goals or its members have concluded that they cannot be helped any further at this time, the counselor may initiate discussion of termination with a reflection such as: "You seem to have run out of therapeutic material" or "Perhaps you have accomplished most of your goals, but you are reluctant to terminate this warm, helpful relationship with these persons whom you value so much."

After they have discussed their feelings and concluded that perhaps this is where they are, the counselor can ask them to consider the following questions: Which of your goals have you achieved? What do you have left to do? For which of these unachieved goals do you require the help of this group? For which do you require individual or group counseling? Who will you select to help you achieve each of these goals and reinforce your learned new behaviors?

For those who have only achieved a few of their goals, the counselor also may suggest questions such as: What could you have done to have made this treatment more productive for you? What do you wish that we would have done differently to have facilitated your learning of your desired new behaviors?

On the other hand, there are some clients who terminate

for the wrong reasons, and usually they do not realize that they could be helped. Such a client quits because he is afraid it will hurt too much to discuss the problem or because he doesn't believe anyone can help him solve it. For him the counselor tries to detect precisely what his motivation to quit is, reflects his feelings as accurately as possible, encourages him to discuss his feelings, helps him explore the consequences of doing nothing in the present and solicits feedback from the other clients concerning his quitting when he could be helped. Sometimes the problem is that the client has not defined his goals clearly enough. Frequently, such discussions result in the definition of new mini-goals or in arranging mini-goals into a hierarchy that can be better implemented, or the development of plans for mastery of skills required to implement new behaviors. On the other hand, some who have not achieved their goals still elect to terminate and do so.

Careful self-appraisal of growth in terms of their own precise, behavioral criteria also can help many clients who did achieve at least some of their goals to discover their own growth and to generalize what they have learned to new situations. Such an assessment can be especially helpful for a client who is stuck on a plateau. During the final session the counselor and clients develop a systematic plan for a followup session (usually about 90 days after termination). This session provides clients with an opportunity to share successes, to be reinforced for their continuing growth, and to generalize learnings to new situations. These sessions also can provide the counselor with feedback that he can use to improve his professional skills.

Closing Ritual

The use of a closing ritual has become increasingly popular with leaders of groups. At least one session prior to termination the counselor encourages each client to prepare for the final session by thinking about which goals he has achieved, on which he must continue work after termination, whose help he will need to continue growing and how he can ask for it, what he liked about other clients' growth, and on what each group member should continue to work ("I urge you messages"). After each client has reviewed his own gains and unfinished goals at the last session, each is asked to stand in front of every other member to receive a good-bye and two final messages: (1) evidence of growth that each client thinks has been especially good and (2) the "I urge you messages." To preserve these messages for the target person, each client is provided with a sheet of paper on which he records separately these messages for his spouse. Many counselors like to use this technique because it focuses attention on each individual's responsibility for his own growth, reinforces goals achieved, highlights each one's need for precise continuing growth, and stresses the idea that one can be helped by one's peers. It also closes the final session on a positive note.

Summary

In order to reap the full benefits of a successful counseling group, clients must learn to say healthy good-byes and to experience closure. When both are done well, clients experience the satisfactions usually associated with completing challenging tasks successfully and the encouragement they need to continue growing. Effective closures also can be used to set the stage for effective followup sessions that enable clients to appraise the extent to which the growth they experienced during counseling was maintained and whether they completed the unfinished business they had when counseling was terminated. Furthermore, effective closure and followup sessions can provide the counselor with important feedback for continued professional growth.

Questions to Think About

1. What do you think a counselor may learn from effective termination procedures that could help him improve his procedures for structuring a marriage counseling group? How could these new procedures help clients define counseling goals? How could they help clients formulate and/or re-write their marriage contract?
2. How would the ways in which a competent counselor terminates a marriage counseling group differ from those of an incompetent or unscrupulous one?
3. What are the negative consequences of ineffective closure

for clients? What are the consequences for the counselor?

4. How can effective closure be used to deal with clients' readiness to accept responsibility for their own growth? How can it be used to determine whether clients have defined realistic goals?

5. How can effective closure be used to help the dependent client? How can it be used to help the monopolizing and/or controlling client?

14

SELECTING A MARRIAGE COUNSELOR

Today there is increasing demand for marriage counseling, marriage enrichment groups, and personal growth groups. Most church-going couples turn first to their clergy for assistance. Although increasing numbers of clergy are seeking some professional preparation in marriage counseling and couples' sexual dysfunctioning problems, most are not adequately prepared to provide all of the professional services they are asked to provide. When this happens they usually can be helpful in locating a professional counselor. School counselors, school social workers, school psychologists, and family physicians are also helpful in this regard. The following professional organizations can be helpful in locating a competent counselor: the American Association of Marriage and Family Therapists, the Family Services Association, regional mental health centers, and state branches of the American Personnel and Guidance Association and the American Psychological Association. Furthermore, the Nader Health Care Group (Adams, 1975) has developed some very useful materials that have helped mental health consumers take more responsibility for selecting and evaluating the quality of services provided by counselors and therapists. With reference to marriage counseling in particular, Koch and Koch (1976) investigated services available and described marriage counseling practitioners, including an analysis of some of the best and worst practices.

> Never have so many couples needed outside help with marital problems.
> Never have so many qualified marriage counselors been available to lend valuable assistance. And yet more than ever before, distressed couples are being fleeced, demeaned, and hurt by inept counselors and by charlatans (*National Observer*, October 30, 1971, p. 1).

Licensure?

There is a growing interest by professionals in licensing counselors and psychotherapists. Those who have sponsored licensure legislation have argued that only respected practitioners in their profession can legitimately define their services, determine what professional knowledge and skills are required to provide their services, develop professional curricula to prepare professionals, accredit colleges and universities that offer these approved curricula, develop standards for ethical conduct, and discipline those who fail to adhere to these standards. In general I agree with this point of view.

Supposedly, licensure laws have been written to protect the public, but too often they protect only the professionals who sponsor these laws. Rarely is an attorney debarred or suspended for unethical conduct or incompetent professional behavior. Even more rarely is an incompetent or unethical physician stripped of his license to practice medicine. Illich (1976) registered concern over consumers' blind acceptance of and dependence on physicians. While Gross (1977, 1978) contends that consumers should accept more responsibility for evaluating all their professional services and for assuming maximum responsibility for caring for themselves, he has also argued for passage of a strong proposed professional disclosure statute that would protect consumers by giving them the information they need to make intelligent choices and provide stiff penalties for counselors who do not adhere to professional standards.

> It [the statute] assumes that accurate information about the service offered by a practitioner is the consumer's best chance of getting what he or she wants and needs and the best protection against harm and exploitation. In effect, it restricts counselors to doing what they say they will do.
> The method by which the statute is to be implemented includes these provisions: (a) Disclosure is to be made to prospective clients before any counseling for which a fee is charged. It is to be legible, on a printed form, and also posted conspicuously, (b) The fact that disclosure is required must be disclosed, including information about the particular department

of government that oversees the procedure so that a complainant would know to whom a complaint is to be made, (c) A notarized form is filed annually or whenever a change in statement is made, (d) Additional disclosure forms are necessary for supervisors and employers, (e) Complaints are made to the department of state government that is responsible for investigation and public hearings, (f) Provision is made for privilege of counselor records during processing of complaints, (g) Judicial review of decisions is made possible, (h) The offense covered by the statute is willful filing of false or incomplete information, (i) Punishment includes the judgment (in several classes) of "misdemeanor" and the prohibition of practice (1977, p. 588).

Some professionals have learned to protect the best interests of the consumer under certain circumstances. For example, some local medical organizations very carefully moni-

I didn't feel comfortable with Dr. Smith. He was too brash and pushy.

Okay; I can accept that. I like Dr. Isaacson. He made some pretty accurate guesses concerning where we hurt. He also seemed to have values similar to ours.

tor the treatment of hospitalized patients and discipline incompetent and unethical surgeons who perform unnecessary surgery or perform it incorrectly. Some bar associations are very active in disciplining unethical and incompetent lawyers. Some local counselors' associations are organized to hear consumers' complaints and to investigate them. Furthermore, where such organizations are most effective, some colleagues have learned to monitor each other. When, for example, a counselor observes a colleague do something that he believes is unethical or inappropriate, he speaks to the colleague about it, and when a client complains to him about a service, he encourages the client to speak directly to the counselor involved, and if he doesn't achieve satisfaction, explains to the client how to register a complaint. If, after discussing the perceived unethical behavior or inappropriate treatment with the colleague, satisfactory resolution is not achieved, the observer reports the behavior to the colleague's supervisor. If the supervisor refuses to do anything about the matter, the observer reports the matter to his local professional organization for an investigation, hearing, and, when appropriate, disciplinary action.

Clients deserve such recourse, and such professional bo havior encourages quality professional practice. Unfortunately it is difficult to achieve because it puts pressure on professionals to be concerned about their clients' best interest and to exhibit the courage required to act professionally. Because too many professionals fail to confront unethical or incompetent colleagues, professionals are increasingly faced with malpractice suits. Were unprofessional and unethical behavior disciplined more effectively within the professions, most complaints could be heard and resolved with clients' help and cooperation.

This problem is not any more serious for counselors than it is for other professionals. However, Koch and Koch's (1976) report suggests that it is a more serious problem for marriage counselors than it is for most counselors.

Professional Preparation

Even for those states that try to protect the public with licensure legislation, the type of public disclosure statute supported by Gross should be adopted. In addition, licensure committees should supplement current written examinations with an oral examination in which a candidate is required to present his qualifications for licensing, including several video tapes of work samples, and defend them. (Those applying for licensure to do marriage and family counseling should be expected to critique video tapes of themselves counseling both families and couples.) Prior to admitting a candidate to such an examination, the licensing committee should seek endorsements from practica and internship supervisors. This practice encourages those who prepare counselors to select candidates with greater care, to practice selective admission-retention during graduate education, to plan and evaluate their students' practica and internship performance with greater care, and, in general, to accept more responsibility for their graduates' professional development. It also encourages followup studies of graduates' performance and continuing professional growth on the job. Most practitioners, and especially the stars, recognize the need for continuing education in order to maintain professional skills, to keep up with research, and to master essential new skills. More stringent screening procedures encourage new practitioners to do the same.

An adequate evaluation of counselors' preparation includes the use of periodic appraisal of their knowledge and skills by carefully constructed achievement and performance tests and periodic interviews during graduate education to appraise their progress, to identify problems with which they may require assistance, and to help them locate resources for resolving these problems. It also includes the end-of-preparation evaluation, which should appraise various components of their program, the working relationships, the teaching materials, the facilities, and the degree to which program objectives were achieved.

Followup visits to each graduate's place of employment also are essential. Most graduate programs appraise students' mastery of knowledge well, and the supervising faculty members try to periodically evaluate the students' development of helping skills, but this type of assessment is much more difficult to make. Supervising faculty must do followup studies to determine the extent to which their graduates actually implement in the field the helping skills that they learned during graduate education.

Except for the clergy and social workers, there is a growing trend for qualified marriage counselors to have an earned doctorate in educational psychology, counseling psychology, clinical psychology, or psychiatry. Most professional organizations have endorsed a minimum two-year graduate program, including such courses as human growth and development, human learning, personality theory, tests and measurements, personality assessment, abnormal psychology, social psychology, research methods, statistics, counseling techniques, group counseling techniques, marriage and family counseling, group dynamics, practica in individual counseling, a practicum in group counseling, and at least one practicum in marriage and family counseling. Usually, enrollees also are required to complete a year of very carefully supervised internship in the type of setting in which they expect to work. In order for a counselor to develop good helping skills, his practica and internship experiences must be very carefully supervised by qualified counselors. Unfortunately, graduate training institutions often do not select practica and internship instructors with sufficient care and do not reward them for doing the careful supervision that is required to produce quality professionals. The example described below illustrates what is required to produce such graduates.

In this practicum for marriage and family counselors, six students were enrolled. Prior to taking the practicum, all enrollees had had two semesters of practica in individual counseling and a practicum in group counseling. All but one had had at least one year of successful experience as a counselor. Each enrollee described the counseling process to prospective clients, selected couples for two couples' groups, and counseled two groups of couples under the supervision of his professor and a doctoral assistant. Each enrollee also counseled one family. Besides individual weekly supervision by both the professor and his assistant, the enrollees were supervised every week for two hours of group supervision during their regular class meeting. Although audio recordings usually were used, enrollees were expected to submit video recordings periodically for both individual and group supervision.

Obviously, the quality of the faculty is crucial. They must be good professional models as well as good teachers.

Client's Practical Guide to Interviewing a Counselor

The following series of questions includes most issues that should concern anyone who is about to enter or is presently receiving marriage counseling. Depending on the answers, the individual should either proceed or seek help elsewhere.

Presentation

1. How did the counselor define the counseling process? Did you understand his description of the counseling process? Was he able to communicate effectively with you?
2. Do you understand what he expects you to do to profit most from his services? Do you understand what you can expect from him and from the other members of the counseling group?
3. Did he propose counseling for you and your spouse together? If not, what did he say when you inquired about being counseled together in a group?
4. How will his services differ from the assistance that you may obtain from an untrained friend or group of friends?
5. Is it clear to you precisely how you can expect to be helped as an individual?—as a couple?
6. Does he appear to be genuinely interested in you?
7. When you spoke, did he seem to be able to give you his undivided attention and to empathize with you—to walk in your shoes—to suffer with you in order to help you discuss your pain and to decide what new behaviors you must learn to function more effectively?
8. Did he seem to understand you and your problems?
9. Did he seem to exhibit confidence in your ability to solve your problems?
10. Did you detect any tendency in him to favor either you or your spouse?
11. When can he see you? How often will he see you? What will he charge for each session?
12. Does his perception of a good marriage seem to agree with yours? If not, do you believe that he will help you achieve the kind of marriage that you want?
13. Does he seem to value and respect you as a human being?

Preparation

1. How did he react when you asked him to describe and defend his qualifications to do marriage counseling? How did you feel about his answers? Was he defensive? If he had little or no graduate preparation, did he seem to try to justify his lack of special graduate education? Did he try to convince you that experience compensates for lack of graduate education?

2. From what colleges and universities has he earned what graduate degrees and in what departments?

3. Which of these colleges and universities has been accredited to prepare counselors? By whom were they accredited?

4. From whom did he receive counseling practica? How were the practica supervised? How were audio and video recorders used in the supervision process? Was he willing to give you the names, addresses, and telephone numbers of these supervisors so that you may seek evaluations of his competencies?

5. What has he done to ensure his continuing personal and professional growth?

6. With whom does he regularly critique audio and video recordings of his counseling sessions in order to improve his skills?

7. After several sessions have been completed, the two of you should sit down and discuss this question: Is he doing what he said he would to help us grow as individuals as well as marriage partners—"truth in packaging"?

Ethics

1. Do you believe that he described his services accurately and that he can actually do what he proposes to do to help you?

2. If you uncovered some problems that he was unqualified to help you solve, do you believe that he would recognize this fact and help you locate another professional who is qualified to help you?

3. Did he help you define criteria that the two of you can use with his assistance to determine after several sessions whether you are making adequate progress? If you decide that you are not making adequate progress, do you believe

he could help you determine what is interfering with your progress and learn to profit from his services?

4. If either of you acted irresponsibly, do you believe that he would know what to do?

5. Does he seem to foster dependency or does he seem to know how to teach you to accept responsibility for your own growth and for reinforcing your spouse's growth?

6. Do you feel that you can trust him—that he will keep confidences?

7. Does he advocate the use of sex surrogates? Has he ever volunteered or hinted at serving in that surrogate role? (Rarely is use of a sex surrogate appropriate. Certainly the counselor should not be that surrogate. Whenever a person perceives another as having more power or control than he, he is not in a position to make a free choice. When, for example, a teacher invites one of his students, or a counselor invites one of his clients, or an employer invites an employee to have intercourse, the latter is obligated to the former and, hence, cannot make a free choice. Therefore, such an invitation is inappropriate.)

8. Have you ever seen him use clients to inflate his own ego or for his own sexual satisfaction?

9. Does he tend to impose his personal values on you or encourage other clients in your group to pressure you to do things that you believe would be inappropriate for you?

10. Is he able to help you cope with others who pressure you to do things that you believe would be inappropriate for you?

Goals

1. What did the counselor do to help you define your own personal goals?—you and your spouse's goals?

2. Did he seem to be able to help you discuss what really worries and upsets you and to develop for each problem specific behavioral goals?

3. Did you get the feeling that he really listened to you and helped you formulate your own goals out of discussion of your own pain?

4. What did he do to ensure that the goals that you and your spouse developed were truly your own goals—not either his goals for you or each of your goals for the other?

5. Was he able to help you develop criteria that you can use to

determine whether you are achieving your goals?

6. Did he help you prepare your spouse to use your criteria to detect your growth and to reinforce it?

7. Did your counselor seem to be able to encourage you to accept responsibility for your own growth and to reinforce your spouse's growth?

8. When you complained about your partner's behavior, was your counselor able to shift your attention from complaining to help you discuss your own deficiencies and decide what you must do about them?

Selection of clients

1. What criteria did your counselor use to select the couples for your counseling group? Did he inform you what these criteria were? Do you think that he used them systematically?

2. Are you satisfied that he selects his clients for his marriage counseling groups with sufficient care? If not, what should he do differently?

3. Did he make the most of the selection process in preparing you for counseling? What could he have done to have prepared you better for counseling?

Continuing Education

True professionals make the most of their learning opportunities while in graduate school and are committed to continuing personal and professional growth following graduation. Employers who are interested in providing good counseling services employ competent counselors who have intellectual curiosity, the potential for growth, and the commitment for continuing growth on the job. They also provide quality supervision of counselors.

Even when good supervision is provided, the professional must take the initiative to ensure his continuing growth. To do this, he must believe in himself and the techniques that he uses and develop a support system that includes some of his colleagues and others who can provide informed, thoughtful help. Moreover, there must be at least one colleague with whom he feels secure in critiquing audio and video tapes and discussing his clients' cases.

A useful columnar worksheet that some counselors have used to critique tapes includes six areas of concern:

1. The counselor briefly describes each of the client's pains (therapeutic material).
2. He transcribes from the tape whatever he said to be helpful in dealing with that pain. If he missed the significance of the pain, he leaves the space blank.
3. He edits the column 2 response and/or writes a new, more productive response.
4. He develops a reflection that relates the client's pain to desired new behaviors (goals).
5. He notes what he said to try to break the client's goals into mini-goals or to decide what he could presently do to initiate desired new behaviors.
6. He records the feelings he experienced as he tried to help this client discuss his problems.

Usually, the counselor is encouraged to listen to his entire tape, complete as many of the columns as he can, and note where he feels that he requires assistance prior to playing the tape for a colleague. In other words, he is encouraged to accept maximum responsibility for his own growth. Critiquing tapes in this manner provides encouragement, feedback, and the support needed to encourage counselors to implement the use of new techniques and to explore new and improved ways of serving their clients.

Best results tend to be achieved when the supervisor emphasizes the leadership rather than the regulating features of supervision. The former stresses support, encouragement, and reinforcement of desired new behaviors, whereas the latter stresses judgment, criticism, and enforcement of the institution's policies. In order for maximum growth to occur, counselors must believe that their supervisor respects them, genuinely wants to help them, and is competent to do so. Positive leadership will do much to accomplish this. Thus, it is important for the supervisor to expect them to provide quality services and to have the courage to confront and discipline those who fail to provide quality services. Under such circumstances counselors feel sufficiently secure to request assistance, to recall and discuss specific troublesome incidents, admit their mistakes, and select from the supervisor's suggestions those which they find most useful.

Summary

There is an increasing demand for marriage counseling, and an increased number of competent marriage counselors, but many sincere clients are being fleeced by unscrupulous, incompetent counselors. Although this chapter encourages the relevant professional organizations to accept more responsibility for monitoring their members' services, it also encourages the public to accept more responsibility for protecting itself. In addition to presenting criteria which prospective clients can use to screen counselors and therapists, the chapter encourages them to sponsor legislation to regulate practitioners more effectively. The self-disclosure act described and endorsed by Gross appears to be one of the most promising approaches for protecting clients. Moreover, it could be used effectively even in those states for which the professionals have insisted on protecting their practices with professional licensure. Finally, the chapter presents ways in which continuing growth can be fostered by the use of self-criticism and proper supervision.

Questions to Think About

1. What do the inept and incompetent marriage counselors lack that the competent ones possess?
2. What are the advantages and disadvantages of licensing counselors and psychotherapists?
3. Why should a prospective client question the competencies of a counselor whose entire preparation consists of weekend and other short-term workshops?
4. What criteria can a person use to evaluate the quality of a practicum or internship?
5. Why should a competent counselor make the sacrifices for post-doctoral internship in addition to good practica and a pre-doctoral internship?
6. What criteria can a practitioner use to assess when he needs further continuing professional education?
7. Why must every profession convey to its clients what they can do to provide feedback to those professionals who serve them and to local professional organizations?

8. Why must competent professionals make it a regular practice to solicit feedback from clients on a systematic basis and on a standard form?

9. In the initial interview how does a client who is apt to profit from marriage counseling behave differently than a poor prospect or a resisting one? How does this client's behavior differ in the first couples' group session? How does this client act in a typical group session?

10. For which of the criterion questions would you want to be most certain about your data before selecting a marriage counselor?

11. What might you do if you felt that your counselor was pressuring you to work on his counseling goals for you?

12. You are a member of your professional organization's state ethics committee and have been asked to investigate the case of a marriage counselor charged with unethical conduct. For what questions on the case would you request information prior to the hearings? What questions would you ask the defendant during the hearings?

References

Adams, S. *Through the mental health maze*. Washington, D. C.: Health Research Group, 1975.

Gross, S. J. Professional disclosure: An alternative to licensing. *Personnel and Guidance Journal*, 1977, *55*, 586–588.

————. The myth of professional licensing. *American Psychologist*, 1978, *33*, 1009–1016.

Illich, I. *Medical nemesis*. New York: Random House, 1976.

Koch, J., & Koch, L. *The marriage savers*. New York: Coward, McCann & Geoghegan, 1976.

Marriage counseling. *National Observer*, October 30, 1971, p. 1.

Author Index

Subject Index

to prospective clients, viii, x,
34–36, 106, 114
Problem identification, 6–7,
10–13
Professional preparation, 182–
184, 186
Psychoanalytic group therapy,
87–89

Qualifications, counselor's, 179–
190

Rationale for marriage counseling in groups, 1–4
Readiness for group counseling,
34–43, 55–58, 63
Reflections, use of, 8–9, 11–12,
94, 154
Relationship building between
client and counselor, 5–7,
8–10
Requests vs. demands, 137,
142–143
Research on marriage counseling, 23–25
Resistance, 40, 41, 100, 106–118,
174
clients' management of,
106–111
counselor's management of,
111–117
group, 111–115
Responsibilities of the client, x,
15, 34, 39, 43, 47, 64, 92–94,
95–99, 103, 106, 117,
134–135,154
Risk taking, 9, 38, 58
Role playing, 9, 12, 61, 69–83, 135
introduction of, 9, 12, 70–71
techniques of, 75–82, 85–86,

98, 112–113, 125, 136, 144,
160
Role reversal, 69–71, 74, 98

Selecting a marriage coun-
selor, 179–190
Selecting clients, 40–42, 188
Self-defeating behaviors, x,
34, 50, 144
Self-disclosure, 63
Sexual dysfunction, 8–9, 11,
18, 21, 57, 120, 132–136
Skin hunger, 27, 132
Soliloquy, 72, 79, 126
Starting the group, 55–58
Structuring, 6, 8, 13–14, 15,
39–40, 42–43, 62, 63–65,
67, 92, 111, 114, 173
Supervision of counselors, 4,
14–15, 92, 99–100, 103,
115–116, 184, 186, 188–189
Support systems, 1, 134, 147,
156, 169, 188

Teaching clients group coun-
seling behaviors, 12,
13–14, 42, 64
Terminating the session, 65
Termination of groups, 115,
173–177
Therapeutic triad. See Triad
treatment model
Transference, 61, 85–103
Triad treatment model, 3, 5–7,
37
Trust, 8, 9, 15, 39, 43

Unfinished business, 7, 26, 69,
73, 76, 85, 89, 109, 173

About the Author

Merle M. Ohlsen is the Holm-stedt Distinguished Professor of Guidance and Psychological Services at Indiana State University. He was Associate Professor (1950–1953) and Professor (1953–1969) of Educational Psychology at the University of Illinois, Urbana. During the 1967–1968 academic year he was on leave as a Roy Roberts Distinguished Visiting Professor at the University of Missouri at Kansas City. Dr. Ohlsen received his B.E. from Winona State College, his A.M. from the University of Illinois, and his Ph.D. from the University of Iowa.

Prior to going to Washington State University (1945–1950) as a counselor educator and college counselor, he worked in the public schools for seven and a half years as an elementary school teacher, a secondary teacher, a guidance chairman, and a senior high school principal.

During 1969–1970, Dr. Ohlsen was president of APGA (American Personnel and Guidance Association). He is a member of ACPA, AHead, ACES, and NVGA. He was a member of the APGA Commission on Guidance in American Schools, chairman of the ACES Subcommittee on Preparation for Elementary School Counselors, ACPA program chairman, chairman of the NVGA nominations committee, a member on the APGA publication committee and the editorial board for *Personnel and Guidance Journal* and *Elementary School Guidance and Counseling*, president of SPATE (1959–1960), and president of the Association of Specialists for Group Work (1977–1978). He was the first winner of the C. A. Michelman Award for his professional contributions to guidance in Illinois, and at the 1978 convention he received the APGA Professional Development Award. He is a fellow of Divisions 2, 15, and 17 of the American Psychological Association, is listed in the National Register of Health Services Providers in Psychology, and is a member of the American Society of Adlerian Psychologists.

Dr. Ohlsen is the author of *The Department Head* (1948), *Guidance: An Introduction* (1955), *Modern Methods in Elementary Education* (1959), *Evaluation of Group Techniques in the Secondary Schools* (1963), *Guidance Services in the Modern School* (1964, 1974), *Group Counseling* (1970), *Counseling Children in Groups* (1973), *Group Counseling* (1977), and numerous professional papers.